"Worry can grow into anxiety, hopelessness ... tivity often overstays its usefulness, it constri... you feel trapped. Let *The Positivity Effect*, Dan Tomasulo's beguiling masterpiece, light your way out. Tomasulo's gift for storytelling makes this an easy read. Yet the true springboards for change are his mind-expanding exercises, each distilled from mountains of scientific evidence. Lean into these to discover the positivity effect firsthand."

    —Barbara L. Fredrickson, PhD, author of *Positivity* and *Love 2.0*

"Dan Tomasulo is one of my very favorite positive psychologists. Why? He is a teacher extraordinaire, and eager to share his knowledge in the most practical, clear way!"

    —Angela Duckworth, professor of psychology at the University of Pennsylvania, CEO and cofounder of Character Lab, and *New York Times* bestselling author of *Grit*

"In *The Positivity Effect*, Dan Tomasulo masterfully integrates rigorous research, captivating storytelling, and practical advice. This book can positively change your life, as well as help you help others do the same."

    —Tal Ben Shahar, *New York Times* bestselling author of *Happier*

"*The Positivity Effect* teaches you how to change the anxiety of transformation into the transformation of anxiety. Using the best of what science offers, Dan Tomasulo gives us the tools to grow in the healthiest way possible."

    —Scott Barry Kaufman, author of *Transcend*, and host of *The Psychology Podcast*

"In *The Positivity Effect*, Dan Tomasulo helps readers transform anxiety and negativity into hope and meaning. Dan blends cutting-edge research with storytelling to offer readers simple and effective tools to help them lead richer lives."

—**Emily Esfahani Smith**, author of *The Power of Meaning*

"*The Positivity Effect* offers the most comprehensive, evidence-based map I've come across for transforming the inner workings of your mind. If you've struggled with negative thoughts, this book is a treasure trove of simple practices and mindset shifts to change your life."

—**Cory Muscara**, author of *Stop Missing Your Life*

"What you have in your hands with *The Positivity Effect* is a masterful set of well-being tools from one of psychology's true master practitioners. Dan Tomasulo will help you unleash your inner HERO. Cherish this book, practice with it, return to it often, and you will likely not only find yourself feeling happier and more peaceful, you'll be well on the road to flourishing!"

—**Ryan M. Niemiec, PsyD**, best-selling coauthor of
The Power of Character Strengths, and chief science
and practice officer of the VIA Institute on Character

"In an area long on advice and often short on evidence, this fun and engaging book teaches evidence-based concepts and practices from cognitive behavioral therapy (CBT) and the science of well-being."

—**David B. Yaden, PhD**, assistant professor in the
department of psychiatry and behavioral sciences at
Johns Hopkins University School of Medicine, and
coauthor of *The Varieties of Spiritual Experience*

THE
POSITIVITY
EFFECT

Simple
CBT Skills to
Transform Anxiety
& Negativity into
Optimism & Hope

DAN TOMASULO, PHD

New Harbinger Publications, Inc.

Publisher's Note

This publication is designed to provide accurate and authoritative information in regard to the subject matter covered. It is sold with the understanding that the publisher is not engaged in rendering psychological, financial, legal, or other professional services. If expert assistance or counseling is needed, the services of a competent professional should be sought.

Copyright © 2023 by Dan Tomasulo
New Harbinger Publications, Inc.
5674 Shattuck Avenue
Oakland, CA 94609
www.newharbinger.com

Cover design by Amy Daniel; Acquired by Wendy Millstine/Jess O'Brien; Edited by Teja Watson

---

Library of Congress Cataloging-in-Publication Data

Names: Tomasulo, Daniel J., author.
Title: The positivity effect : simple CBT skills to transform anxiety and
    negativity into optimism and hope / Dan Tomasulo, PhD.
Description: Oakland, CA : New Harbinger Publications, [2023] | Includes
    bibliographical references.
Identifiers: LCCN 2023000800 | ISBN 9781648481116 (trade paperback)
Subjects: LCSH: Positive psychology. | BISAC: SELF-HELP / Personal Growth
    / Happiness | SELF-HELP / Anxieties & Phobias
Classification: LCC BF204.6 .T663 2023 | DDC 150.19/88--dc23/eng/20230310
LC record available at https://lccn.loc.gov/2023000800

Printed in the United States of America

25   24   23

10   9   8   7   6   5   4   3   2   1   First Printing

This book is dedicated to my granddaughter,
Josephine Grace Fetrow

Contents

Foreword

What if you were given a high throne, from which you could issue much of your lot in life? Your scepter could point away from a life full of struggles with negativity, to instead oversee a world replete with gifts of positivity. You could issue forth a personal agenda of happiness, joy, and hope. Or, from this point of impact, you might toss your life into suffering, emotional pain, and nihilism.

The wisdom in *The Positivity Effect* by Dr. Dan Tomasulo, a leader in the field of positive psychology, puts you in this seat. You may have yet to enter this chamber within your own inner life. But it is waiting for you: the empty chair saved only for you. Dr. Tomasulo gives you a map to it, the key, and a guide to the range of decisions that you might make, looking out from your seat of personal power. While no human being has total control of outward events, each of us is built with the internal point of awareness to exercise choice in how we perceive, focus, interpret, and ultimately act in response to these outward events. Dr. Tomasulo even goes on to show that, in time, our awareness can budge some of the so-called outer events—particularly when it comes to the quality of our relationships, the use of our innate talents, and the forces of our persistence and effectiveness in the world.

Dr. Dan Tomasulo is a teacher extraordinaire. He has risen to be academic director of Spirituality Mind Body graduate studies at Teachers College, Columbia University. Here, I have seen him *live-action* teach hundreds, perhaps now thousands, of Columbia University students over the past ten years. As a skillful guide, Dr. Tomasulo will also introduce you to your own inner seat of awareness. From up there, you are empowered to exercise a great measure of choice over your "take" on things, or cognitive appraisal; your "emotional life," or mental embrace; and with practice, to develop a new "M.O." for living!

If you say yes to trying out these inner practices, you are handed a great deal of liberation. Having positivity inside your mind means that no longer are you tightly emotionally tethered to life's unwanted, shocking, immediately painful outward events. You are free to live the life you want to live. Only you can determine your level of inner positivity. This choice is readily detected by everyone who surrounds you: your work colleagues, life partner and children, and even the fellow in the next seat on the train.

We can raise high a bright torch in dark times of total night; or we can slump toward the ground with dissatisfaction on a sunny day. How do you want to live?

Knowledge is power. Dr. Tomasulo empowers you by handing you some of the best insights in the field of positive psychology. He writes in an encouraging, clear, accessible voice on some of the most important research findings in psychology, when it comes to choosing your emotional lot in life. He builds mnemonics to help you remember your way to a seat of positivity. He chronicles an actual human life who, through inner choice, flourished after confronting catastrophic evil—Holocaust survivor Viktor Frankl. He then shares peer-reviewed studies revealing our shared human ability to make life-affirming choices in times of collective trauma, such as 9/11. The possibility to face tremendous adversity, and make ourselves *more rather than less*—more caring, more connected, more hopeful—is shown through the established body of research on post-traumatic growth.

Dr. Tomasulo wants you to live your best life. A life driven by *The Positivity Effect*. The vision and execution of your first-rate life are within your control if you look from the right vantage point. Such a life is found not merely in the events that come your way, but in your choice of whether or not to sit upon your own inner throne, hold court with your key people and events (good and bad), and ultimately choose a reign of joy.

—Lisa Miller, PhD
Professor and Founder, Spirituality Mind Body
Institute, Columbia University Teachers College,
and author of *The Awakened Brain* and the
New York Times bestseller *The Spiritual Child*

INTRODUCTION

Find Your HERO Within

A hero is an ordinary individual who finds the strength to persevere and endure in spite of overwhelming obstacles.

—Christopher Reeve

Do you wake up with your to-do list breathing down your neck? I used to. The list of things I needed to do, hadn't gotten done, or had forgotten about altogether seemed to be waiting there for me every morning. Each day brought new issues to deal with, and the list of what needed to get done (or redone) seemed to grow. The little things were building up—and so were the stress and anxiety. I found more distractions. It became harder to focus, and harder to complete tasks. It was hard to find even a little space to breathe, with too many deadlines, too little sleep, and too much caffeine.

If your own stress and anxiety have become a daily battle, you are not alone. Worldwide, anxiety is crippling—and is the leading cause of limiting a healthy life.[1] In the United States alone, more than 40 million people over 18 have some type of anxiety disorder. Countless more have chronic stress and anxiety that may not be diagnosable but are still difficult. Stress and anxiety are gateways that lead to depression and physical conditions. If you have significant anxiety in your life, you are five times more likely to have medical issues that need a doctor's attention. What's more, people with anxiety disorders are six times more likely to be hospitalized for psychiatric disorders.[2] Anxiety is our greatest obstacle to well-being.

Yet there is hope—even empowerment, resilience, and optimism—in the pages of this book.

Millions of us are on edge, worried, and anxious, and the need for relief is burgeoning. While most of us manage to get through the day, the week, and the crisis at hand, something is always bubbling below the surface, ready to hijack our thinking. Yet only about a third of the people with significant stress and anxiety in their life go for treatment.[3] Why is it that anxiety is both widespread and undertreated?

People with anxiety are more likely to go to a doctor,[4] a general practitioner, internist, or another specialty than to a psychiatrist or psychologist. They are looking to make the anxiety vanish. On one level, this is good news, because they are looking to treat the condition. At another level, this may also be part of the problem, because they do not necessarily seek the help of a mental health professional. If the root of the anxiety goes untreated, it can become more intrusive.

The bodily symptoms that come from anxiety include heart palpitations, muscle aches and tension, shaking, sweating, shortness of breath, and insomnia. They can also include fatigue, difficulty concentrating, chest pain, jaw pain, rashes, stomach problems, and even persistent hiccups and tinnitus—ringing in your ears.[5] These symptoms tend to drive us to the medical doctor—a person trained to alleviate the physical signs (usually with medicine) but not trained to treat the causes of the mental or psychological aspects of anxiety. So many people who go for treatment are going for the *symptoms* of the anxiety—not the *reasons* behind it.

But we know that when something is not treated at the core level, it is likely to return. This is particularly true with anxiety and depression. People tend to take the medicine their general physician prescribes—usually an antidepressant, which can also alleviate anxiety symptoms—for a while. It works a bit, but then they stop and the symptoms return.[6] Even more concerning, research shows that nearly 70 percent of these patients never actually met the criteria for clinical depression, and nearly 40 percent were being treated for anxiety symptoms when they didn't meet the criteria for an anxiety disorder.[7] There are a number of reasons this approach isn't working.

Research on this has been thorough. Irving Kirsch of Harvard Medical School examined data from a number of independent studies, to determine the overall trends[8] when it comes to the effectiveness of antidepressant medications. Dr. Kirsch's research shows that the medicines used to treat depression and anxiety may help when they are first taken, yet they do not prevent recurrence of symptoms. Essentially, science has clearly shown that if people feel better and stop taking the medication, the same symptoms return.

In other words, the treatment works only if you keep taking it. Taking medicine to reduce your anxiety doesn't help to heal or prevent it— instead, it helps you rely on the drug, with all of its side effects, to keep anxiety in check.[9] It is important to note that I am not saying the medicine can't be helpful. It is, but it has long been known that the major antianxiety medicines, benzodiazepines, help to reduce anxiety but lead to dependence, toxicity, and abuse:[10] they work to reduce the anxiety temporarily, but never get at the cause. This can be described as *treatment* success with *sustainability* failure. When asked whether the medicine is effective, my answer is: yes and no. Yes, during the treatment phase. No, when it comes to healing the cause.

If any aspect of stress and anxiety has generated fear, uncertainty, or ambivalence in you, you may not have sought help in the first place. Whether you have only gotten treatment relief (perhaps from an antidepressant or antianxiety medication) or have been unwilling to try any treatment at all, I understand you may be hesitant. You may not be—you may be ready to try something new—but if hesitant is how you are feeling, it is understandable. You may feel ashamed of not having control of your feelings, be afraid of being labeled with a disorder, lack belief in the effectiveness of any treatment, fear side effects of the medicine, be concerned about addiction or dependence on the medicine, or simply need to learn more about how treatment works.[11] Although anxiety is extremely common, you may be among those who fear a stigma associated with mental illness, or the consequences of a diagnosis. You might assume you cannot afford treatment, think you can handle it by yourself, not know where to go for treatment, or even believe you'd be forced to take medicine.[12]

With all these considerations, it's not surprising that many people do not go for treatment at all. As a result, they may struggle with hopelessness, or feel that they have no sense of agency around their future. This feeling may be keeping them stuck, unproductive, and trapped in a downward spiral of negativity. Let's look at this downward spiral more closely before we explore the way out.

The Science of Negativity

Science knows a lot about how we worry. A loop in our brain begins with a negative thought, followed by not seeing a way to positively impact the future. The concern about the future creates greater anxiety or worry, which then causes feelings of hopelessness—generating more negative thoughts.

The Tony Award–winning musical *A Strange Loop* portrays this powerfully. The main character, Usher, interacts with a cast of his own negative thoughts as he considers his future. As Usher tries to get out of this loop, his personified negative thoughts (*You don't know what you are doing, You can't do this, Who do you think you are?*) show up with more frequency and intensity.

Negative thinking seems relentless. This is because negativity comes from an invisible fountain of anxiety and worry. Yes, the demands of our outside daily life press on us in ways that make our inner life difficult. But what science has learned is that the stressors themselves don't influence us as much as the repetitive negative thoughts that follow. As Thoreau reminds us, it's not what we look at that matters, it's what we see.

Do any of these negative thinking traps sound familiar?

I'm not good enough.

I know I'll mess up.

I'll never be able to manage my anxiety.

I'm too old.

I'm not lucky.

I should just give up.

Anything less than perfect is a failure.

I messed up—now everything is ruined.

I'll never become what I want to be.

I'm not strong enough.

I'm too young.

I should be better than I am.

I can't do anything about it.

Others think I'm stupid.

They don't like me.

Nobody cares.

Nobody loves me.

I always make mistakes.

I should never make mistakes.

I'm stupid.

I'm a loser.

I'll faint.

I'll go crazy.

I'll freak out, and no one will help.

I'll make a fool of myself and be embarrassed.

I can't win.

It's too late.

How could I do that?

I'm not smart enough.

No matter what I do, things won't change.

What's wrong with me?

I may as well die.

I can't control my feelings.

I'm a failure.

I can't do this.

Notice which ones echo in your mind—and especially, the ones that are repetitive. In chapter 2, we'll target these first, because negative thoughts are the biggest roadblocks to well-being.

The relentless inner world of repetitive negative thoughts is like a whirlpool. It keeps you stuck in one place, all the while pulling you down. When this happens for a long enough time, your inner frustration can turn outward, toward others:

I can't believe they're like that.

What is wrong with them?

They shouldn't have done that.

That's not right.

What are they doing?

I'll have to do it by myself.

In the end, we criticize others, ourselves, or both. The cycle feeds on itself, without much of a pause.

We have survived as a species because we've learned how to worry— we have a proclivity toward worrisome thoughts that scientists call a *negativity bias.* Humans are drawn to worry about what might hurt us in some way. Over time, we have given more and more emphasis to worry, and positive emotions have become little more than frivolities. We don't linger on them. Typically, after experiencing joy or a sense of connection with others, we go right back to worrying about the next thing on our list. The result is that the negativity walls can close in, as a trap of anxiety ensnares us. This is more than a vicious cycle—it's the trap that becomes our life.

This book can help free you. Here's how.

The Choice: True Freedom or Seductive Trap?

In their effort to help you, most medicines, psychotherapies, and coping techniques have targeted the reduction of stress and anxiety symptoms. Therapists and physicians try to minimize these problems, but is trying to minimize their effects the only way to alleviate your suffering?

The science and practice of coping are focused on alleviating suffering by reducing the symptoms. Most therapists and physicians have been trained in the science and practice of coping: working to reduce symptoms. Drug companies are in line with this approach, which says, if we treat the symptom and lessen its effect, the patient is cured. In fact, if you look at the history of medicine and psychology, the research and practice approach has focused almost exclusively on symptom reduction, correction, and recovery.

Further, a lot of effort has been put into combining the best of what medicine has to offer with the best of what psychotherapy has to offer. The thought is: if we combine the efforts to reduce symptoms, we'll get better results. This is what most mental health professionals recommend and is supported by the research. Toward this end, one of the leading medical journals recommends using antidepressants and cognitive behavioral therapy (CBT) to treat stress and anxiety. They make this recommendation because both medication and CBT work to lessen the symptoms. Many researchers consider CBT the best treatment for anxiety and depression. Using meta-analysis studies (large-scale studies that look at many other studies on the same issue), about 48 percent of adults achieve some remission[13] (discontinuation of symptoms) and up to 45 percent of youth under 18 get good results.[14]

But CBT has the same relapse problem as medication. Studies show that CBT is also effective for many during the treatment phase, but once the treatment stops, more than half will relapse within the following year—four out of five within the first six months.[15] When professionals combine the two methods, antidepressants and CBT, the results don't get better. When measured by relapse—what happens *after* treatment rather than reduction *during* treatment, these joint interventions still do not work well enough. The average success rate of the treatment phase— what really worked—still hovers around only 50 percent, and the relapse rate is even lower.[16]

If each of the methods alone is only partially effective, and together they don't improve the permanent situation, what can be done? Alleviating suffering is certainly a noble goal, but focusing only on symptom reduction doesn't work very well because symptoms come back once treatment is over. Over time, simply continuing the treatment, if it is medicine, can create problems of side effects, dependency, ineffectiveness, and potential addiction. Psychological interventions, when continually used to reduce the symptoms, also become ineffective, if they were ever effective at all.[17]

Something new is needed—a different approach, a different measure of well-being. It is not enough to have a treatment take away the pain for some people for a short period of time—only to have them relapse. We need something more sustainable that offers more hope and faith and focuses on the vitality that comes with fully healing.

The major meta-analysis (those large-scale) studies agree that to help people fully heal their problems at the root, we need better treatment interventions that lessen relapse.[18] More-effective treatment interventions require a different way of thinking about the problem. So, let's apply a different lens to anxiety.

The Science of Thriving, Flourishing, and Well-Being

In the last 20 years, there has been a shift in psychology away from looking at the importance of alleviating suffering. Instead, many are now looking for ways to increase well-being. This new emphasis is under the general umbrella of *positive psychology*, and the specifics of how it is applied are referred to as *positive psychotherapy*.

This approach can empower you to make changes by helping you experience more positive emotions—and, at the same time, teaching you to reduce negative emotions. Studies around the world show over and over again that increasing well-being may be the most effective way to reduce negativity.[19] This focus on increasing your positive emotions while using your strengths is emerging as the most successful and efficient tool to reduce experiences of stress, worry, and anxiety.

This is a radically different approach to well-being. Symptom reduction is only half the job—adding specific interventions to improve positivity is the other half. Research has shown that decreasing negativity without simultaneously increasing positivity is a losing battle.

This is because negative and positive thoughts are typically *unbalanced* when we are under stress and worried. Imagine that negative thoughts are like pebbles, and positive thoughts are like feathers. The question is: Can the feathers ever balance out the scale? Can they tip it in the direction of positivity? The short answer is yes—but you need *a lot* of feathers.

Medicine and traditional therapy approaches knock the negative thoughts off the seesaw and keep the pebbles from piling on. *But they don't add more feathers.* As a result, while you might come back into balance, even a grain of sand can tilt the scale so that negative emotions and anxiety dominate once again. You may relapse because there isn't anything positive being added to the feathers' side. You need to add more positive emotions, by using your strengths.

In this way, positive psychology can offer the other half of the equation. The approach suggested in this book is designed to work in tandem with medical and traditional therapeutic approaches. We want to add the findings of positive psychology to the toolbox—not try to replace other tools.

When a pebble gets tossed on your scale, it is essential to become more empowered to remove it—and to learn how to add more positivity at the same time. This leads to resilience, meaning we successfully adapt to a difficult or challenging life experience and begin, as leading resilience researcher Dr. George Bonanno says, "a stable trajectory of healthy functioning."[20]

This approach is very dynamic because as you are working to keep the pebbles from accumulating, you are also looking for and learning how to gather more feathers. Once you know how to balance the scale by removing negative thoughts, you keep them at bay by adding more positivity.

The science and tools of CBT can now be amplified, extended, and enhanced by tapping into the research on activating our strengths and positive emotions. In a private communication before he passed, Aaron (Tim) Beck, the founder of CBT, expressed gratitude to Dr. Martin Seligman, founder of positive psychology, for adding positive emotions into the future path of research for CBT. The science of what we know how to do is always better informed when a creatively different approach is also applied. In this case, the fresh approach is to cultivate the causes of well-being.

Types of Well-Being

Science has learned that your well-being can have a permanent effect on your physical and mental health.[21] In life, there are four types of capital that contribute to well-being: financial (what you have), human (what you know), social (who you know), and psychological (who you are).[22]

- **What you have** relates to the material resources you have at your disposal, like money and tangible assets, or material goods.

- **What you know** could be your knowledge, skills, training, ideas, or education.

- **Who you know** through social capital refers to your relationships, friends, and network of connections.

- **Who you are** is psychological capital, which is what *The Positivity Effect* is all about.

To shift well-being in a positive direction, there are four different emotional skills needed. Collectively, these four resources are known as *psychological capital*, or *psy-cap*, which consists of:

Hope: *Choosing* to believe you are in control of the *future*, to act with agency

Empowerment: *Capitalizing* on *past* successes, to build confidence

Resilience: *Cultivating* a flexible mindset in the *present*, to build readiness and courage

Optimism: *Converting* how you explain the *past* and expect the *future*, to gain perspective and certainty

These skills are sometimes referred to collectively as HERO.[23] Each of them relies on the essential skill of *self-regulation*. Note that I have chosen to use the word "Empowerment" rather than the original E proposed in HERO, "self-Efficacy"—a belief in one's capacity to influence a situation, typically one's sense of confidence.[24] Because empowerment is considered a predictor of self-efficacy,[25] it is better suited to this book.

This book is about giving you access to your inner HERO. You will learn specific ways to cultivate hope, facilitate empowerment, develop resiliency, and promote optimism. We all have these resources, but they are often untapped because they have not been given the emotional nutrients needed to thrive. The key to unlocking the power of psychological capital is learning self-regulation, which means regulating your perception. Perception can directly change your emotions and your experience into something more positive. Here's what to expect along the way.

How You Can Experience *the Positivity Effect*

As you read this book, you will learn about the new science surrounding HERO. You'll be invited to engage with practices, to learn to become more hopeful, empowered, resilient, and optimistic. Through evidence-based and evidence-informed interventions, you will be able to keep pebbles from accumulating in life and add more feathers.

Chapter 1 teaches you how to see differently. In order to eventually change what you think and feel, you have to first change what you are looking at and what you see. A brief assessment will help you understand how you currently view positivity and negativity in your life. You'll also recognize the patterns of seeing that have become habitual. An exercise is introduced to help you learn how to break these habits and start seeing and responding to the world afresh.

Chapter 2 reveals the new science of *hope*, which has the power to change our interpretations. In this chapter, the emphasis is on understanding the differences between hope, faith, and optimism—and appreciating the unique opportunity of hope. Hope is the only positive emotion that requires negativity or uncertainty to be activated. The core hope skill is learning to shift your perception away from assessing something as negative so that you can attend to different aspects of the event or situation. This allows you to interpret it anew and see it in a different, more hopeful way.

Chapter 3 is a crash course on our brain—how it works like a search engine on a computer, and how *empowered* people have learned how to hack it. This chapter dives into the research and practice of how accessing more positive emotions helps you plan better for the future, how self-care is the best way to begin and maintain an upward spiral, and how all of this leads to confidence.

Chapter 4 emphasizes how responding *resiliently* to the unexpected is important in determining outcomes. Just like the GPS in your car, when life detours you, the route toward your destination may require a reappraisal. Chapter 4 teaches how to respond effectively to a difficult situation by developing a flexible mindset and learning how to take a truly mindful pause, a technique developed by Dr. Ryan Niemiec.

Chapter 5 shows us the dramatic outcome of *optimism*, believing something good can happen. For better or worse, the degree to which we expect and believe that something will occur greatly influences our experiences and outcomes. You will learn how to borrow positive emotions from your future by learning to think about your Best Possible Self. You'll also learn to develop an optimistic mindset.

Chapter 6 gives you ways and reasons for acting differently in the world, by understanding three ways you can sustainably enable your future. The first is through learning more deeply about your ability to self-regulate, with a technique specifically designed for coping with obstacles. Second, you will explore the phenomenon of *post-traumatic growth* (PTG) and learn how to grow tremendously following a traumatic experience. Finally, you will learn about how the adaptive, harmonious forms of passion can help your well-being.

To keep track of your progress through these chapters, I encourage you to keep a notebook—either handwritten or digital. I'd like you to notice what happens when you do these explorations, so that you can assess their effects. If you can, do the exercises when you are prompted to. I know it's tempting to keep reading and do them later, but doing them as you go has been found to be effective and will give you a real sense of what it's like to shift your perspective and regulate the way your brain processes information. This will support the journey mapped out in this book, and your notes will remind you of what has worked and how. When I have used examples and case studies to illustrate a technique or make a point, the names have been changed, along with any identifying details, to protect the identity of the individuals.

The positivity effect happens when the percentage of positive thoughts, feelings, and behaviors becomes sustainably greater than the negative. Your inner HERO is about to be awakened, but there is something important for you to know before we continue. You are not getting ready to start the program—*you have already begun*. If you have gotten to this point, I admire your *courage* to begin, *curiosity* to stay engaged, and *persistence* to continue. Courage, curiosity, and persistence are your strengths, summoned to the challenge.

Take a moment to reflect on this. You're already demonstrating these traits, and likely have not yet noticed them. But they have been with you all along. They indicate your belief that change is possible, and that you've regulated your perception. You're already on the path toward making the positivity effect happen.

I admire these traits because they represent the natural gifts you bring to the situation. They are your feathers, and there will be more.

Let's go find them.

CHAPTER 1

You Can Transform the Negativity of Stress and Anxiety

The question is not what you look at, but what you see.

— Henry David Thoreau

In the 1984 movie *The Karate Kid,* the lead character, Daniel, needs to learn how to defend himself against high school bullies—so he learns karate from Mr. Miyagi.

Mr. Miyagi has Daniel come to his house, and for days has him engaged in repetitive menial chores like waxing his car. Mr. Miyagi instructs Daniel to apply "wax on" to his car in a circular clockwise motion with his right hand, and "wax off" counterclockwise with his left. After days of doing these routine hand movements, he develops a series of defensive blocks through muscle memory. This eventually helps him become a karate champion. Initially, Daniel didn't understand how essential repetitive learning was going to be to his success.

The ability to transform your thoughts also requires repetition. Just like Daniel in the movie, if you don't develop a basic discipline for transforming your perception, you can't improve. However, you will be developing emotional—rather than muscle—memory. You can think of this habit of positivity as "wax on," whereas preventing the temptation to interpret things as negative is "wax off." We need both of these basic skills. This chapter focuses on how you can begin by actively looking for things that bring peace and joy.

Overcoming the Landslide of Negativity

The number of thoughts we have per day is reported to be about 6,000.[26] It was previously reported that 80 percent of our thoughts are negative.[27]

This leaves most of us with a staggering amount of nearly 5,000 negative thoughts per day. We are creatures of habit and are drawn to the familiar, and if the familiar is negative—negativity will return.

Every time you worry about getting something done on time, paying a certain bill, dealing with a difficult person, or worrying about an upcoming deadline, test, or presentation, a pebble is added to the negative side of the balance. If you repeat the thought—as the research suggests we do—you add another pebble. Rumination becomes a landslide of negativity pebbles on your scale.

Now imagine you have a positive thought and corresponding feeling. A friend is coming to see you on the weekend, and you are looking forward to it, or a long-awaited check came through. The positive thought and feelings would go on the other side of the seesaw.

But, as mentioned, the positive thoughts and feelings wouldn't be the size of pebbles—or even the size of crushed gravel. They would be feathers you'd be adding to the other side. If the above statistics are true, each day we would put 5,000 pebbles on the one side, and about 1,200 feathers on the other. No contest.

Even if the number of positive and negative thoughts were equal, the negative would still outweigh the positive, due to the negativity bias. Because of this, approaches that only limit the number of pebbles we put on the scale don't work. Four thousand pebbles rather than five thousand won't create a shift—we're still going to relapse. But what if we could bring that number of negative thoughts all the way down to 10? Just 10 pebbles a day. Surely that would make us feel better, yes?

Not necessarily. This is like saying that the bullies are picking on you seven times a day versus two. Yes, this is an improvement—but the situation hasn't really changed, and you remain at risk. It won't matter how few pebbles you have on the one side if there isn't a sufficient volume of feathers on the other to outweigh the anxiety, worry, and negativity.

Research has shown that a primary way you can facilitate resilience (successfully adapting to a challenging experience) is by increasing positivity.[28] We'll take a deeper dive into this in Chapter 4, but for right now, the important understanding is that reducing worry, anxiety, and negative thinking alone won't bring about sustainable change.

Nothing will work until positive thoughts outweigh the negative. *Nothing.* Please take a moment to realize what this means. Stopping negative thoughts *isn't enough* to prevent them from returning. The thought bullies are still going to steal your lunch money until they learn they can't threaten you. Once they know you aren't threatened—because you have lots of powerful friends, your positive emotional feathers—they lose power over you. The scientists call this shift toward having more hope, empowerment, resilience, and optimism *affect balance*, because it is the balance shifting toward more of the positive that will make the difference.[29]

EXPLORATION: Your Emotional Scale

What if you were able to measure every thought that passed through your mind? What if, on a given day, it was possible to determine how many positive versus negative thoughts you had? Imagine you could put, on a scale, the negatives on one side and the positives on the other. What would your scale look like? It might look something like the one on the following page. Compare the words on either side of the scale and write in your journal those that generally best describe you.

Add up the ones on the left side (your pebbles) and then the ones on the right side (your feathers). If you have four or more on the left side of the scale, you are likely to tip in favor of the negative—even if the other side has twice as many positives, the scale won't balance. This is what we are up against. But the science and practice tell us this can change—and it can change rapidly.

Pebbles		Feathers
Worried	or	Curious
Disturbed by others	or	Engaged
Feeling at fault	or	Emotionally sturdy
Nervous	or	Ready
Angry/disapproving	or	Fulfilled
Unprepared	or	Grateful
Easily distracted	or	Paying attention
Resentful	or	Insightful
Apprehensive	or	Emotionally passionate
Unwilling	or	Thoughtful
Mostly struggling	or	Mostly satisfied
Fearful and afraid	or	Loving and caring

To Activate Positivity, Look for It

There are three things you are working toward to achieve a balanced emotional scale: reducing the number of negative thoughts, increasing positive thoughts, and then, when you get good at it by improving your core skills, learning to move the fulcrum point so that positivity tips the scale.

Know that one great big feather isn't going to tip the scale—mostly because there are no feathers that large. If you have 5,000 pebbles a day on one side, you'd need a feather the size of Manhattan to even come close...and you'd need one every day. You may be like most people and believe that when you get the dream job, the supportive partner, the substantial raise, the luxury car, or the beach vacation, the scale will tip in a positive direction.[30] Unfortunately, this isn't true. While the great thing you finally get may give you a temporary mood boost, soon afterward the rumination of negative thoughts will return, making your life anxious and stressed once again.

So how do you bring more positivity into your life on a regular basis? You begin with a review, a search, a savoring, and an honoring of all the positivity that is already around you. You won't be able to find positive emotions in your life at the frequency you need unless you look for them. Let's take a deeper look at how you might start your own mental version of "wax on."

Research shows that once people can activate a positive feeling, there is a natural tendency to want more of it.[31] Importantly, for the purpose of this exploration, studies show that being able to pick out something positive from among the negative is particularly vital.[32] For example, if you notice a smiling face within a sea of disgruntled ones, or the beauty of an urban community garden in the midst of an expanse of concrete, it can elevate your experience. When you deliberately look to increase your positive emotions, scientists call it "upregulating." Here's a chance for you to try it.

EXPLORATION: Look for Peace and Joy Right in Front of You

Even if you are in a crummy mood and are worried about a number of things, you can still look for the positive. The good surrounding you can get lost in the negativity. You need to make a deliberate effort to retrieve it and amplify it. By focusing on the available peace and joy, you will start plucking feathers out of the rock pile.

We are going to begin right where you are—in this moment, with whatever is in front of you. Look around you. In your journal, create three columns.

- Label the first column "Object." Here, make a list of things, objects, or images that bring you joy or a sense of peace. Make a list of a minimum of 10 things.

- Label the second column "Reason." Write the reason why this object brings you peace or joy.

- Label the third column "Memory" and write what the object evokes from your past.

Here is my chart in this very moment.

Object	Reason	Memory
Laptop writing desk	Gift from my dear friend	Our deep friendship
Coffee mug	Purchased from a favorite diner	Cozy feeling and food
Handmade tray	Gift from another friend	Our newly developed friendship
Flourishing begonia plant	A purchase from the local florist	Initially spotting its beauty
Cast-iron plant stand	Repurposed and refinished from an old table	Pride from restoring
Electronic notepad	Huge help in organizing	Vast improvement from my old method
Small slate patio	Waited years to be able to afford it	The moment of inspiration
Old table	Finally fits perfectly where it is	Places I tried this table before its current home
A handmade sign	Gift from my partner	Recalling the thoughtfulness of the gift
My laptop	Purchased after a job promotion	Thrill of getting chosen for the job

Now, write down any themes you notice in the lists. For me, the thing that jumped out was how people close to me have given me gifts that I enjoy having around me while I am working. I wasn't fully aware of this before the exercise.

Being able to notice your surroundings, and the peace and joy that are already there, awakens your senses, memory, and gratitude for what you already have. This pause for positive thought allows you to notice, appreciate, and amplify it. Savor the positive emotions connected to your present moment.

Searching for, and shifting your perception toward, what is already positive begins to add lots of feathers to your scale. This exercise demonstrates an axiom from happiness pioneer Tal Ben Shahar: "When you appreciate the good, the good appreciates." In this beautifully crafted quote, Dr. Ben Shahar has captured the essence of why scientists study upregulating. When you *deliberately* focus your attention on things that are more positive, you expand your awareness. In doing so, you can see more possibilities for positivity. This shift is the difference between looking at a snapshot and looking at a panoramic view. When you start to notice the good in the snapshots of your life, it creates an opportunity to expand your perspective and find a panoramic way of seeing situations.

Just like a craftsman learns to use tools of their trade in acquiring mastery, each chapter gives you new tools to work with to develop your skills in mastering psychological capital. The tools are meant for you to integrate into and continue using in your life. They are not one-off experiences. They are the *repetitive habits of perspective* that will begin to change not only how you see the world, but how you then participate in it. So continue to make the three-column charts and look for the positive—that which brings you joy and peace.

You can even fill out the positivity chart when you're in a sour mood or stressed, or things have gone wrong. As you'll quickly find, when you cultivate the positive while the difficulties of life swirl around you, it is precisely your negative experiences that can elevate your capacity for gratitude. As Shaun Hick has said: "You need to spend time crawling alone through shadows to truly appreciate what it is to stand in the sun." We'll continue to explore this throughout the book.

Now that you've learned the basics of "wax on" positivity, let's turn our attention to "wax off"—reducing the anxiety, worry, and negativity that hold you back.

CHAPTER 2

HOPE: Act with Agency by Believing in Your Future

One's destination is never a place, but a new way of seeing things.

—Henry Miller

Do I have time to take a walk before it rains? Where should I go to eat? Does this shirt look okay? I don't know if I can take a vacation then. Can I get the paper done by the deadline? Can I make the train if I leave now?

If your day is like mine, the unknowns are endless, and uncertainty about the future is pervasive. We are constantly making decisions about what to do, how to do it, and if it can be done at all. It is in this space of uncertainty that hope lives.

Hope is the first of the traits in HERO, for good reason. The new understanding of and research on hope are proving that it's a tremendous untapped resource of well-being. *Hope* is often used interchangeably with terms like *faith* and *optimism.* However, over the last few years, the research on hope and hopefulness (which I use interchangeably) has evolved radically—including a more-scientific study of the three dispositions of hope, faith, and optimism.

Each disposition is measured differently, to note its occurrence and activation, and while there is overlap, it has become clear that hope is different from optimism and faith in the following ways:[33, 34]

- Optimism is a *general* expectancy that good things will happen in the future.

- Faith is the expectation that some *greater force* will make these good things occur.[35]

- Hope is different: It is a belief that a positive future outcome is possible, *combined with a desire for that outcome.*[36] This means there is something *you can do* specifically to control the future.

Neither a general optimistic wish nor a faithful relinquishment of responsibility to a higher power is as effective as hope for transforming negative thoughts and feelings, because hope is the belief that we can make change happen.

These understandings, and a wealth of research, have taught us a great deal about hope's nature as a uniquely positioned positive emotion. It is so effective because of how it is aroused. Hope is the only positive emotion that requires uncertainty or negativity to be activated. This means that hope uses the raw material that can lead to worry, anxiety, depression, and despair—and converts it into a motivational force for change. Hope has the ability to transform obstacles into opportunities, problems into possibilities, and setbacks into challenges.

Hope can be thought of as having different outcomes when applied to business,[37] medicine,[38] education,[39, 40, 41] meditation,[42] character,[43] psychotherapy[44]—and even climate change.[45] There is nothing quite like it throughout our lifespan.[46] It is unique because it engages our conflicts, hardships, obstacles, and difficulties—to our advantage. How does it do this? If you'll pardon the analogy, hope takes the manure that shows up in our life and uses it as fertilizer to grow magnificent things.

Just as manure enriches the soil with beneficial microbes that encourage micronutrients, hope is a catalyst for growth. No other positive emotion needs discomfort to be stirred into action. Hope is triggered by the despair that can come from negativity or being uncertain. Through hope, obstacles become like fertilizer, enriching the soil of your life.

Tolerating Uncertainty Opens New Possibilities

Negativity and uncertainty deliver the element of hope, which is essential for your well-being. Without difficulties to cause negativity and uncertainty, you won't produce enough hope to awaken the strength of your character. Like plants that flourish and thrive when manure is spread on them, you become stronger in who you are as a result of the challenges you face.

As far as positive emotions go, hope is the human ability to adapt to challenges. It is woven into the histories of what has helped people survive and overcome significant setbacks, limitations, and even trauma in life.[47] Hope provides us with the ability to be flexible and motivated to change.

Hope is defined as a *belief that a positive future outcome is possible,* combined with *a desire for that outcome.*[48] Significantly, this definition lacks one notable aspect: *How* does one achieve this belief?

In the book *Learned Hopefulness: The Power of Positivity to Overcome Depression,*[49] I emphasized cultivating hopefulness through the regulation of perception. Learning how to challenge our perception allows for different, and usually better, ways of understanding circumstances. This is how our beliefs are crafted and nurtured. "When we change the way we look at things," as Dr. Wayne Dyer said, "the things we look at change."

Have you ever been uncertain which path to follow, choice to select, or decision to make? You wouldn't be human if you hadn't. In fact, being ambivalent is our most common state.[50] But if we stay too long in the state of uncertainty, this natural and common part of being human turns destructive.

Intolerance of uncertainty—the tendency to react negatively to uncertain situations—has been shown to be a specific characteristic of persons with generalized anxiety disorder (GAD).[51] It has been demonstrated both in specific types of research involving CBT treatment[52] and in meta-analyses.[53] In other words, it is a proven fact that uncertainty unravels us—particularly when we struggle with anxiety.

Hope's unique feature of needing negativity or uncertainty to be activated gives us access to this core issue of intolerance of uncertainty for people with GAD. Instead of our experiencing debilitating uncertainty, hope can harness the agitation of chronic uncertainty through its transformative ability. Think of it this way: Wind, water, and the sun can cause property destruction, flooding, and skin cancer when untamed. Yet we can derive tremendous benefit by learning how to convert these potentially destructive forces into energy sources. In the same way, hope can change the intolerance of uncertainty into a source of great power. Let's look at how this works.

Riva is an actress I worked with. She regularly auditioned for roles, and was having a run of particularly painful rejections. The regularity of her work slowed down tremendously, and then stopped altogether. She became anxious and depressed, and for nearly a year she was highly uncertain about remaining in her profession. Although she had been a professional actress, singer, model, and dancer since childhood, with Broadway, TV, and movie credits, she deeply questioned what to do with her life.

This profound uncertainty about her future took its toll. Her intolerance of this uncertainty generated so much anxiety that she could not find meaning or purpose in doing anything. She stopped eating, socializing, and taking care of herself.

To help her understand how hope works, the first thing she had to embrace was a paradox: that wishing for the situation to improve, while simultaneously wanting to get out of the profession, was causing the uncertainty and anxiety to get worse. It was perpetuating the ambivalence, because she was pulling herself in two directions: giving herself conflicting messages of "I want to stay" and "I want to leave."

This is where hope can exert its magic. Agitation and lack of progress come from the desire to go in two directions at once. Like setting the front wheels of a car in opposite directions, there can be no forward movement until they are aligned. At heart, intolerance of uncertainty is a lack of alignment between goals and motivation. Hope offers the solution: recalibration.

First, Riva needed to accept the situation for what it was—a given. Then, she asked how the energy caused by the agitation of uncertainty could be used as a source of power. Since she had time now and no prospects with her acting, she decided to take her skills as an actor and train as a drama therapist, returning to school to become a licensed social worker. She took out a school loan, returned to school to earn her degree, and set out on her second career. The moment she stopped worrying about what she couldn't do, her anxiety lifted, confidence returned, and she started landing major roles in television and movies. She now balances her beloved but unreliable acting career with her stable career as a therapist.

Riva looks back at her anxiety during that time of transition as the necessary catalyst for change. Once she moved toward the conflict, rather than avoiding it, she was able to heal the anxiety. Hope transformed her situation by regulating her perception, recalibrating what she needed to do, and then moving her toward, not away from, the conflict. The potentially destructive wind in her life filled her sails. Importantly, Riva was over 40 years old when she made the transition in her life.

Hope Is Found by Shifting Perception

When something uncertain or negative comes about, there is a moment when the event and your interpretation of it intersect—and at that moment, meaning is made. You've interpreted what has happened, and your response is determined by the reaction *to the interpretation*, not *to the event*. What influences your understanding has a great deal to do with your habits of explanation and context.

To explore this, think of a time when something was bothering or upsetting you for a while. Because of that ongoing experience, it can become harder to see the world positively. Things that you might usually interpret as good get cast in a negative light. Say you are behind on a project and become anxious about it. Then a friend calls, who wants to go out. You are worried and nervous about the project, feeling overwhelmed by the task and the deadline you missed. You see your friend's request, which is usually very welcome, as a potential intrusion. Something that is typically pleasant becomes an encroachment on your time. Your negative reaction has nothing to do with your friend's request and everything to do with your interpretation.

In the mid-1950s, research was done that began exploring how this interpretation phenomenon[54] worked. It is known as a *perceptual set*, and it means that what we see is a matter of our readiness to see it. Now, take a look at this image.

A

12   13   14

C

What do you see when you look at the figure in the center of this illustration? It depends. The interpretation of it relies on the context. You will notice that the two lines near each other in the middle look like a *13* when looked at from left to right, and a capital letter *B* when scanned top to bottom. The perceptual set makes it a number or a letter—two completely different interpretations—depending on how you look at it. Read right to left and you'll see the numbers *12, 13, 14,* but read top to bottom and you'll likely see the letters *A, B,* and *C*. In this case, you are influenced by a type of expectation, either a letter or a number, depending on the way it is approached—from either the number *12* or letter *A*. As a whole, we are influenced by how it is viewed in context.

A positive or negative reaction works in the same way. Just as we are prepared for a number or a letter because of what comes before, our interpretation of events is influenced by expectation and context—which are then used to justify our perception. However, change the cues—look at it from the top down rather than side to side—and we see something different. How we regard the friend who wants to go out will change with the context. They are an awesome friend when we're bored and a pest when we're overwhelmed with an overdue project. We derive meaning from the context. In this way, positive or negative reactions (our pebbles or feathers) are created mainly by our expectations—our anticipated perception of them.

For Riva, the situation of not having work as a professional actress was initially seen as B. The lines were top-down and the interpretation of them was to see the situation as unwanted, a loss, and yet wanting outside forces to change it. Through our work together, as she came to understand hope, the same lines in the middle were interpreted as the number 13, not the letter B. The time became an opportunity to use her well-developed skills in a new way, setting different, recalibrated goals that aligned the situation with her ability to take action. In this way, the same situation shifted from being an obstacle into a possibility. The two lines in the center of her life didn't change, but Riva regulated her perception of how they were going to be interpreted.

Finding Your Way When Lost in Rumination

Sometimes the context of a situation leaves us at a loss for meaning. It is hard to interpret something that we cannot understand. Imagine looking at the chart if you know only Mandarin Chinese or the Cyrillic Russian alphabet and numerals. The two lines that can be seen as a 13 or as a B might not have any meaning at all. Likewise, there are times when you have to figure out what an event means for your life but can't settle on an interpretation.

The source of uncertainty can come from not knowing which is the best way to perceive something—or from the fact that we can't correctly determine the context. The uncertainty would generate both a deep engagement *and* frustration. You would be captivated and upset at the same time. This is what causes rumination—the repetitive, recurrent, persistent, prolonged negative thinking about one's self, feelings, concerns, upsetting experiences, and ongoing uncertainties.[55, 56]

Rumination is at the very core of worry and anxiety. Researchers have identified that it is the essential factor in what keeps us stuck. It does this in a variety of ways—such as magnifying and prolonging bad moods, making us vulnerable, keeping us unwilling or unable to change, blocking therapy efforts, and increasing physical stress responses. We struggle to figure out what to do while imprisoned by our thinking. We get too lost in our thoughts to be able to act.

Sometimes the negative thoughts are coming from a real and scary threat. Even so, our perception of that threat determines a lot about how we respond to it. Let's consider what we've learned from the COVID-19 pandemic.[57] Researchers determined that two things happened when people had a negative mindset (a "negative affect balance") about the threat of COVID-19: 1) a negative mindset heightened the degree to which they felt threatened, increasing their negative mood; and 2) this created irritation and nervousness, which were brought on by feeling the threat of the virus. In the researcher's own words: *"Thus, there was a circular relationship, in which perceived threat influenced the presence of negative mood, and negative attitude, in turn, linked to emotions of irritation and agitation from a present situation, promoted the feeling of threat."*

This shows how perception is at the very center of a vicious no-win cycle. Our perception of how vulnerable we are both influences and is influenced by our mood. (There is much more on how we can use this feeling of vulnerability to our advantage in Chapter 6.) In other words, *the degree to which we are uncertain is regulated by what we feel, and what we feel is affected by our uncertainty.* Perception affects our mood, and the mood we are in changes our perception. If we are in a negative mood, it will generate a high degree of uncertainty (in the COVID-19 study, this was labeled "vulnerability"). If we are highly uncertain ("greater perceived threat" in the COVID-19 research), it will generate negativity. No wonder negativity can pull us into a downward spiral.

I once got lost in China during one of my trips to give a series of lectures. I set off from the hotel to find Tiananmen Square. I don't speak Mandarin but was guided by my cell phone's translator and easy-to-read color-coded maps for the subway. During the day, my phone was fully charged, and I made my way there easily. As the day grew into the night, and I got dinner and did some more sightseeing, I got lost. My cell phone's battery died, so I could not find a subway nor translate to ask for directions. The symbols all around me that I so desperately needed to find my way were suddenly sources of uncertainty and anxiety. What could provide comfort and clarity couldn't be interpreted.

If you can tolerate uncertainty, you will generate less anxiety. The ability to endure unsureness and ambivalence buffers the uncomfortable nervousness. You can handle the apprehension from the uncertainty, so you give yourself more time to think clearly. A different perspective of the situation can emerge, a solution can materialize, or support can arrive.

When I was uncertain about how I would get back to my hotel, I was able to regulate my perception. I did it with hope: by shifting my anxiety toward the *belief that a positive future outcome is possible,* and feeling *a desire for that outcome.* I was hopeful because I could not imagine I would never get to my hotel and never return home. The belief was that I could control this aspect of my future. I had no idea how that would happen, but this uncertainty, this obstacle, awakened a positive sense of challenge.

When a difficulty can be perceived as an opportunity to be creative, persistent, and energized, hopefulness is ignited. The uncertainty of the situation generates anxiety, which is converted into motivation to solve a problem. Just as in Riva's case, the situation doesn't change, but what we do about it does. Hope is a catalyst that transforms uncertainty into solution-focused problem-solving.

In China, I tried several ways to get back to the hotel. First, I looked for someone who spoke English, which proved unsuccessful, as each person I approached either shook their head or shrugged their shoulders. Then I looked for charging stations for cell phones but couldn't locate any. I tried to hail a cab using my limited capacity to explain where I wanted to go—which was not received well by the cab drivers. Ultimately, it occurred to me that I needed to first find a place where people spoke English and could help me access transportation.

When you can align your anxiety with an attainable goal, this reduces your anxiety and you begin moving toward a solution, rather than remaining stuck. I found a hotel where the kind people at the front desk spoke English, explained where I was on a map, that trains weren't a good choice from my location, and arranged for a cab to bring me back to my hotel. When you can align your reduced anxiety with an attainable goal, you shift the destructive force of rumination into an aligned motivation.

Discovering the Source of Your Struggle

So, what happens if we just cannot shift our perception, find hope, and feel motivated to meet the challenge? When our ability to tolerate uncertainty is low, we can deplete our *coping capacity*, the cognitive and behavioral ways we manage internal and external stressors.[58] This means that as we find our resources diminished in one arena, we become depleted in another. Once uncertainty goes unmanaged, it drains our reservoir of what I like to call *hardiness*, a term researchers used to call resilience. Over time, we become less and less able to manage, more overwhelmed, and the frustration can take over. When you feel drained, you often do not have enough resources for yourself—or others.

This is what happened to Natalie, who came to see me for her anxiety and angry outbursts.

Natalie was anxious most of the time. She had frequent headaches, stomach pains, and trouble falling or staying asleep. Natalie was "somewhat occasionally happily married," with two children, but was lately on edge with everyone. "It seems that I'm not happy with anybody these days. The closer people are to me, the nearer they are to my wrath," she said. Natalie's attention to detail was evident in her perfectly chosen outfits—revealing a need for perfection and control rather than style. Before our work together could truly begin, she needed to consider that she might be unhappy with herself and that the conflict wasn't on the outside, but on the inside. As our sessions continued, Natalie realized how each disappointment, battle, misunderstanding, frustration, and angry outburst had one thing in common: She was uncertain about what to do in a situation.

Whenever uncertainty arose, first she judged herself, then others. When I offered the possibility that she was judging herself around various uncertainties, it seemed to be both a truth she embraced and a burdensome reality. Yet focusing on this truth became a turning point in her therapy. We emphasized what was happening inside—not the external conflicts.

"It sounds like you are very critical of others," I began. "In almost every instance we have spoken about—with your kids, your friends, your husband, your boss—you are judging them, and before you lash out at them, there is a struggle, a judgment going on, inside you. It makes you anxious. You are criticizing yourself, uncertain and upset about not being able to control the situation, angry at them for not helping you get control, and then angry at yourself for feeling that way. You're caught in a loop of some kind," I offered. "Does that sound right?"

Natalie looked at me for a longer than usual time. Then, she finally said: "People *have* mentioned that I am a control freak," she said, wrinkling her nose. "And I guess that's what you are saying too, right?" She continued, not waiting for an answer. "That I can't seem to control the thoughts I am having on the inside, where I am *constantly* uncertain and judging myself—what I should have done, what I didn't do, and what needs to be done. But instead of dealing with those thoughts, I'm lashing out at others, to try and control them since I can't control myself."

"I wouldn't say you're a control freak," I said with a smile. "Around here, we say *control enthusiast*."

Natalie burst out laughing, maybe a bit more than the joke warranted, appreciating the release. It was the first time she realized that her internal struggles had created a negative lens through which she was looking at the world. If we are uncertain of how to handle a situation and critical of ourselves, we will be critical of others. Her anxiety was coming from a constant stream of internal confusion and criticism.

Like Natalie, once you understand where the source of an issue is coming from, you can turn your flashlight on it so that it can be dismantled. But first, let's explore the nature of that flashlight.

EXPLORATION: An Observer of Your Life

We all have an inner flashlight that shines on our experience. This is our awareness watching what is happening, all the time—even when we are asleep and dreaming. There is a part of you constantly monitoring your thoughts and feelings and behaviors. It's a lot like watching TV. To practice being aware of this self-observer, answer the following questions in your journal.

- What did you have for breakfast? (awareness)

- How did it taste? (observation)

- How did you feel after you ate? (effect or impact)

The fact that you can easily answer these questions reveals the part of you that is like a camera, watching you go about your day—and in this instance, eat breakfast. That observing self is with you all the time. It is the part of you that is keeping track of what's happening, by noticing with awareness, observation, and a sense of the effects or impact. Now that you have your flashlight ready, we can turn it on the negative thoughts that fuel your anxiety.

Learning where an oil spill is coming from and repairing the issue at the source works better than only cleaning up the beaches. So, with your flashlight, let's look directly at the source of your negativity. Later, we'll explore how this power of observation can change negativity to positivity, using hope.

EXPLORATION: Seeing Your Negative Lens

Let's go back to the list of negative, repetitive thoughts I shared in the introduction to this book. I will ask you to do what I requested of Natalie: Identify the top three. To illustrate, I'll show an example.

First, pick the first of your three that you want to work with. In this example, I will use Natalie's most disturbing thought: *I should be better than I am.* After you've chosen yours, please write it down in your journal. Then, alongside it, write what your internal witness sees—your observer, and the feeling or impact it has. Create a chart that looks similar to this.

Repetitive Thought (Awareness)	What Happens (Observation)	Feeling (Effect or Impact)
I should be better than I am.	I am judging myself.	Demoralized

Now become curious about the observation. Negative thoughts are almost always judgments.

As I explained to Natalie: "When this thought comes into your mind, there are two points of view happening at once: the belief causing the distress the *I'm not good enough* thought—and the self-observing witness—the flashlight—that recognizes the distressing feeling."

Natalie said, "I think I am only aware of the one that believes *I'm not good enough*. It's constantly telling me *I should be better than I am*."

"I agree, and that may be part of what we want to change," I countered. "That the negative belief causing you anxiety and negative thinking are the only things you are noticing. But that means there is a part of you noticing it."

This was an important awareness for Natalie to have, because it meant understanding that the thoughts and feelings that say negative things like *I should be better than I am* are being monitored by another part of yourself. The you that is observing is like the you that watches a TV show. You have chosen the TV channel and are watching what you've selected. It might be an enormous screen with very loud speakers, but you choose the channel, its content, and the volume.

A repetitive, negative thought is like choosing a horror movie on a wide-screen TV, turning the volume up, and watching it over and over—complaining all the time that you don't like the movie. The thing is, you can change the channel at any time.

This might come as a revelation. Often the negative feelings are so strong they hide the fact that they are a part of your consciousness that is being observed. Like dark clouds that eclipse the sun, they can make you forget that there is a bright sun still there that can help them evaporate. When you are learning to transform negative thoughts, you are certainly aware of them, because you hear them constantly. But now, you can realize that these thoughts are being observed by another part of yourself. This can be an awakening.

EXPLORATION: Get Curious about How Judgment Hurts You

The easiest way to transform a judgment about ourselves or others is to change the observer's point of view from judgment to curiosity. Becoming curious rather than judgmental can transform the feelings from negative to positive.

In your journal, answer this motivation question: *What makes me keep thinking* [fill in your own repetitive thought]? Then observe the effect or impact of each answer.

Here are Natalie's responses. Like her, you will most likely notice that these judgmental interpretations result in negative feelings or impact.

Motivation	Judgmental Observation	Feeling (Effect or Impact)
What makes me keep thinking I should be better than I am?	It makes me think I am not as good. It keeps me quiet and from saying something stupid.	It keeps me distant from others. It protects me from humiliation.

But when there is curiosity, the answers can change. Once the judgmental interpretation is removed, there may be other reasons this repetitive thought is happening.

Motivation	Curiosity Observation	Feeling (Effect or Impact)
What makes me keep thinking I should be better than I am?	It motivates me to try harder. It lets me listen and learn.	It inspires me. It teaches me to have humility.

Now create a sentence that combines the judgmental observation with the negative feeling or impact. You can use this template:

When I think _____, it causes me _____ and this keeps me _____ and it _____.

Here is what Natalie wrote:

When I think I should be better than I am, *it causes me* to stop from saying something stupid *and this keeps me* distant, protects me from humiliation, *and it* demoralizes me.

This was the horror movie Natalie was watching, day in and day out. She seemed trapped by her own thoughts that were making her feel bad. So I asked her, and I'll ask you: If you want to change the show you are watching, how do you change the storyline?

"Change the channel," is what Natalie said and what most people say.

But that's not what people *actually* do with negative thinking. They take the TV apart to tell the characters to change their scripts. The judgment keeps them looking in the wrong place to make change. This doesn't work and makes them anxious and depressed and causes the distress they experience.

The truth is, you have the power to change the channel, to watch a different show, and you're not doing it. We all have that power. But when the movie absorbs you, it can be so scary or overwhelming that you can forget you're watching it and be totally absorbed in the drama. The key is to remember that the power is inside of you—not the TV. You are the observer—and if you don't like what you are watching, there are other channels to choose from.

Knowing there is another option and then learning to experiment with that, makes all the difference. We realize change is possible, which gives us hope. As Riva did, Natalie had to reinterpret her situation. In Natalie's case, the *B* was that other people were the cause of her anxiety and anger. The reframing, seeing her *13*, as it were, was to recognize that she had more control than she realized over the situation.

EXPLORATION: Changing to a Positive Channel

Here is Natalie's Curious Observation chart again. Hope is knowing a positive shift is possible. Let's look at how this can work.

Motivation	Curiosity Observation	Feeling (Effect or Impact)
What makes me keep thinking I should be better than I am?	It motivates me to try harder. It lets me listen and learn.	It inspires me. It teaches me to have humility.

We are not trying to stop the negative thoughts from arising. Instead, we're trying to correct them when they occur. A good way to do this is to look at the language you're using for motivation. The next two steps will show how to change the language.

First, create a sentence that combines the specific positive thoughts that could create the desired impact. You can use this template:

When I think _____, it motivates me to _____ and this keeps me _____.

Here is the example from Natalie:

When I think I should be better, it motivates me to try harder, listen, and learn, and this keeps me inspired, humble, and encouraged.

Second, check the language of the motivation. Often, the judgmental observation is queued up by how the motivation is presented. When Natalie reviewed her motivation, the word "should" jumped out at her. She saw it as a type of judgment and felt it implied she was doing something wrong already. For Natalie, a less judgmental motivation was swapping out the word "should" with "can." She took the repetitive thought and modified it with one word.

When I think I should be better, I need to change it to I can be better.

What can you do with your motivation statement to make it less likely to trigger a judgmental observation?

Try to make your statement as concise and essential as possible. Here is the template:

When I think _____, I need to change it to _____.

This is the work of hope. Changing "should" to "can" may seem like a small thing. Yet it is these very targeted responses that help make the transformation. By noticing where the leaks are in our psyche, we know right where the healing needs to take place. As Leonard Cohen so eloquently put it: "There is a crack in everything. That's how the light gets in."

You can be ready to challenge negative thoughts by using their positive essence. This means taking what they are striving to accomplish, and applying it to your advantage. To do this, use a corrective sentence. You can use this template:

When I judge myself by thinking _____, it is an opportunity to remind me _____.

Here's an example:

When I judge myself by thinking I can be better, it is an opportunity to remind me of the motivation to listen and learn—and my desire to be inspired, humbled, and encouraged.

To discover hope, Natalie used the negativity of *I should be better* to pinpoint where the correction was needed—just as a cut on our finger, or a splinter, tells us exactly where to focus treatment. In much the same way, you must know where to apply the healing that hope can bring to a situation. Hope is like the antibiotic ointment you put on a cut to keep it from getting worse while letting the natural healing properties happen; it is being applied to make the future better, by first not letting the cognitive wound get worse. Hope then facilitates the expectation that the future will be better because of something you've done directly to help it heal.

The Upward Spiral

Remember the research on COVID-19, which showed that there is a circularity to negative thoughts and moods? The reverse is also true. Research has shown that positive emotions increase the odds that people will feel good in the future, by broadening their awareness. This is due to the fact that as we increase our awareness, we become more aware of options.

What helped Natalie shift was, at its core, a broadening of her awareness to include her observing self. Once she realized she was watching a channel she could change, this awareness was enough to nudge her to feel hopeful. In a circular way, the awareness allows for more options, which in turn can change our perception of a situation. This can result in a positive shift in mood, which then allows self-generated positive emotions. Perception, in this way, affects a positive mood. Indeed, these effect studies show that life satisfaction goes up, depression goes down, and this cycle continues to create an upward spiral.[59]

For better or worse, mood and perspective will shift our perception. Let me end this chapter with a story about one of the most hopeful people I know—someone who let the light in. As a freshman in college, Kathryn learned her father had committed suicide. This news unraveled her. "The pain was something I couldn't even comprehend," she explained. "I thought it might kill me, so I did everything I could to get through it, yet I just couldn't handle it. I had spent the first 18 years of my life trying to make my dad happy, and I did not know who I was without him."

This trauma led Kathryn to have to deal with her own depression and anxiety, while struggling with addictions and self-hatred. She felt like an utter and complete failure and would find herself in deep states of anxiety and major depression. Essentially, she would ruminate herself into a depressive episode.

Then one night, in her cabin in Wisconsin, she had what she described as a "brain attack." Battling addictions, eating disorders, a divorce, financial problems, weight gain, a serious illness, job changes, not having kids, PTSD, and family challenges, Kathryn found herself face-to-face with all the pain she had buried deep within her soul. In a surge of panic and pain, she attempted suicide. In what many might call a near-death experience, Kathryn says she looked down on herself and saved her own life. This was when she found hope.

"I can't tell you the amount of times I have experienced deep, persistent hopelessness," she recalled. Hopelessness is the single most consistent predictor of suicide and is defined as both emotional despair and motivational helplessness. So, to save her own life, she had to start proactively managing her emotional despair and motivational helplessness. She needed to stop running from her feelings and start embracing them. She needed to start letting them fuel her purpose and learn how to go from helplessness to action.

Kathryn learned that not only was hopelessness predictive of suicide, but it was predictive of violence, self-harm, addiction, partner violence, risky behavior, absenteeism, weapon-carrying on school property, and more. And hope was predictive of all positive life outcomes.

So now she works on herself. *Every day.* It is a simple construct, yet not easy. It takes practice. Work. Diligence. Some days are better than others. She works on generating positive feelings first, and only then gets to inspired action.

Her suicidal ideations aren't gone. Yet when they arise, she asks herself these questions, and you can too.

- *What am I hopeless about? (If I am feeling hopeless about many things, I can decide to work on one that I can tackle.)*

- *How can I manage the despair? Express my anger, sadness, and/or fear?*

- *How can I activate positive feelings?*

- *What one action can I take (knowing that sometimes the most powerful action is just to not take action)?*

- *Who can I turn to for support?*

- *What thinking challenges are most getting in the way of getting back to hope? (Am I trying to control things outside of my control? Am I internalizing a failure? Am I ruminating? Am I worrying about the future? etc.)*

She goes through this process each and every time she feels hopeless, about anything. And she always finds her way back to hope. "It is literally unbelievable to me. Things I think might feel so bad they kill me, don't. I let myself cry when I need to. Bawl. I get into it. And it doesn't last forever—I always thought it would. And then I do something healthy, to increase the dopamine and oxytocin in my body. I exercise. I focus on how I want to feel, and I do things that generate that."

Kathryn doesn't panic anymore, and she now speaks around the world. She is an entrepreneur and strategic consultant, and was appointed to be a representative at the United Nations for the World Federation for Mental Health. She is the innovator behind Mood-lites, a brand that achieved over $35 million in retail sales, and this success helped Kathryn launch the first nationwide marketing campaign for mental health. She founded iFred, the International Foundation for Mental Health, and created the first free global program to teach young kids how to hope, Hopeful Minds. She is working to activate hope through Hopeful Cities. Through her company, Innovative Analysis, she now teaches how to have a hopeful mindset, no matter what life brings. As Kathryn says:

I've turned all of my experiences into beautiful lessons, and I use them to serve others. I believe we are here to experience wonder, joy, and awe, as much as possible. And I love turning all the trauma and pain into healing, insight, wisdom, and support for others. Our emotions are what make us beautifully human. And it is in learning how to use those hard emotions in service of the world around us that reveals what we care most about. We all have a gift, all of equal value and profound importance, and life is simply a process of learning how to transform those gifts to elevate us all.

In the first chapter, we discussed the beginning of adding feathers. This chapter taught us how to change the negative channels we tune into—which helps reduce the number of pebbles, while adding feathers. In the next chapter, we'll look at ways to empower ourselves—tipping the scale in favor of positivity.

CHAPTER 3

EMPOWERMENT: Feel Confidence as You Build on Success

The greatest weapon against stress is our ability to choose one thought over another.

—William James

When I began this journey into the power of positive psychology, I was skeptical. I couldn't imagine how noticing the things around me that bring me joy, or changing words in my head from "should" to "can," could have any lasting impact. At best, these techniques seemed trivial and too gentle to generate true change—at worst, they struck me as a waste of time.

If you are skeptical, please remain so. The only way these principles and interventions work is when your willingness to experiment allows for a new experience to challenge your existing thoughts. Stay skeptical until the experiences invite you to take a different position. Most people who believe in the power of positive psychology have had some experiences, as I have, that proved its value. So stay open to observing its effects, and keep reading to learn more.

The principles of positive psychology must become self-evident through your interventions, in order for changes to take place. More classic styles of psychology would have approached changing stress, anxiety, and negativity by attempting to reduce these symptoms. The positivity effect uses positive emotions as a catalyst for enduring, positive change. Moving away from ruminating negative thoughts is only part of the work. Not relapsing, and then learning how to thrive, were components missing in psychology—until now. As you learn to gather more and more feathers, the scale tips favorably and consistently in your desired direction.

Whether you are skeptical or a believer, you have the power to choose how you think about the material in this book. That is the point of this chapter—having the power to choose your thoughts, and the power to change that choice if it is not working for you. As we make our way through HERO, we come to *empowerment*. Empowerment and the confidence that results from it require understanding how the thoughts you choose get selected, and then hacking into that system so that your preferences support your well-being.

Confident people see themselves in a particular way because they have made a choice. This *decision* is about how they are going to perceive and think about who they are now—and in the future. Choosing how you are going to think might sound outlandish. But thoughts follow in the direction of our attention. What you pay attention to becomes your truth—and then becomes your future. Confident people pay attention to certain elements in their life, which sets the stage for them to think about the future differently. Confidence is about perception.

Searching Your Experience for Answers

Let's begin this exploration by looking at what happens when you plug in key words to begin a search on the Internet. If I want to know *how to cook fish,* the key words are *cook* and *fish,* and anything that has those tags would be flagged. The sites that get the most hits come up at the top of the results list. For this search, the very top result was about how to cook codfish, with recipes, spices, and a host of easy-to-make codfish dinners.

I don't like codfish, and that wasn't what I was looking for. But now I have more information about codfish than I wanted, all because the algorithm says this is the site that has the most hits. What I really wanted was an answer to a different question, but I phrased my question too generally, so the results reflected high frequency—not specificity.

I'm sure you've had this experience on the Internet, and you probably instantly realized how to correct it. You needed to give the search engine a more specific request, with clearer key words. What I really wanted to know was *how to cook tuna fish on a barbecue grill*. The results yielded 71,000,000 hits, offering answers to exactly what I wanted to know. On the first try, not a single one did.

The answer to my question was there, on the Internet, but the results depended on the way I asked. If I didn't ask a clear enough question, I got information I didn't need, and no help for my situation.

Now let's look at the search engine in our brain. It is known as a *default network* (DN). This is what the brain uses when it is passively selecting and internally organizing material.[60] To illustrate, let's unpack the process of what happens when someone asks you: "How was your day yesterday?" To answer a memory-related question like this, the DN search engine in your brain immediately heads out on a path to look for answers.

Just like the search engine on the Internet, as the DN starts to look for all the information about yesterday, it is also going to pull up the material that has the greatest number of hits. The negativity bias I described in the introduction tends to draw attention to itself—to what it believes we need to be worried about in order to survive. This means negative and uncertain thoughts tend to get more hits.

The DN search tries to answer the question "How was your day yesterday?" based on the number of choices made in the past. Research shows that during a maladaptive cognitive style, such as depression, the DN would be mediated by rumination.[61] This is to say that the DN search to answer a general question like "How was your day yesterday?" isn't random. When your mind has been focused on anxiety, fear, and depression because you are ruminating about it, your brain's DN search engine produces results that are negative memories, or thoughts with a negative tone. It thinks that is what you are looking for—and so the answer about your day is negative.

Overriding Your Default Search Results

If you are passive and allow the DN to lead the way, you are likely to get negative results. But you can get much more powerfully positive answers and feelings when you look for the good things that are already there. You have the power to choose your answer to a question like *How was your day yesterday?*

Here is my default response to the question: *Mine was miserable. I found out I owe more taxes than I had planned for. After waiting three days for the plumber to come to fix the toilet, it broke again an hour after he left. The place my partner and I wanted to have lunch at was closed because they lost electricity. My Internet went out during a Zoom call. My daughter called to say that the visit she and the family were planning couldn't happen. One crummy thing after another.*

Let's try this again. The exact same day could be answered through a different lens, a positive one: *Mine was fabulous! My partner and I took a long walk on the beach, and when one place was closed, we found a new restaurant we hadn't tried that was wonderful. My friend asked me to have dinner with him, to celebrate his daughter getting into her top-choice university. I got asked to speak on a very popular podcast and invited to give a keynote. A gift came from a former student, of a book she'd recently published, and my son-in-law invited me to do a bike race with him. One fantastic, joyful thing after the other.*

Both answers are true. All the experiences happened within the past 24 hours. I could truthfully answer the question either way. The difference is in what I intended to retrieve.

The way in which you choose to recall the details changes how you feel, your understanding of events, and your expectations about what will happen to you in the future. It is important to understand what happens when those choices are made.

Choice gives shape to our thoughts. Similar to an Internet search engine, the DN will respond differently when we ask it to look for something specific. How we retrieve our thoughts determines what gets recalled, and the way—positive or negative—in which it is retrieved.

Molding Your Thoughts for the Future

I like to think of thoughts as being like water. Water takes the shape of a container in the same way that thoughts take the form of our choices. If I make a choice to look for kindness in the world—kindness is the container I fill with my thoughts. They take on the shape of kindness. But if I choose to look at times when I've been betrayed, my thoughts take on the form of betrayal. We choose what we agree to attend to—and our thoughts follow.

A friend gave me rubber molds that make round ice spheres rather than cubes. I enjoy the round shape but must remember to take the deliberate action to put water into the sphere mold. If I mindlessly fill up the normal ice cube tray, I'll get what I always get—rectangular cubes. But if I remember to put the water into the shape I want, I get what I like. Same water—different outcome. The difference is the form chosen. Your thoughts, like water, are molded from the containers you put them in.

Just for fun—say, if this book were titled *The Negativity Effect and How to Achieve It*—what do you think I would be encouraging you to recall about the day? Let's say you wanted to know how to become more miserable and were looking for a surefire way to make that happen. I'd begin by asking you to highlight and detail all the worst parts of the previous day. I'd ask you to make a list of all the things that went wrong, focus on them, and then repeat and remind yourself of them as often as you could.

I'd emphasize that anxiety is the best pathway to fear,[62] and that recent research shows that anxiety and fear about COVID-19 increase psychological distress while simultaneously reducing life satisfaction.[63] As a bonus, you would learn that uncertainty and doubt from these fears and anxieties would fuel pessimism about the future.[64] You would learn that the more choices you make about the negative things you remember, notice, and brood over, the more miserable you would feel.

I'd encourage all these things because I'd want you to feel empowered in your ability to achieve your goal of chronic misery. If the goal was to give you the confidence that you could make yourself miserable any time you want, I'd offer exercises on how to cultivate doubt, worry, and fear.

I know all of this sounds ridiculous. But with a little practice, focusing on the negativity and uncertainty in your life *would* help you create a dismal outlook. By learning to focus on the negative, you would start to see results immediately, and within a month you'd have tipped the scales consistently enough to experience the negativity effect. You would be miserable almost all the time.

Of course, this is a silly example because you wouldn't deliberately want to make yourself feel worse. But this is exactly what happens when people live with chronic anxiety, fear, and depression. Research shows and science has revealed a strong link between rumination, negativity, and uncertainty—and reduced life satisfaction and well-being. All of which lead to increased pessimism.[65] People who ruminate on the negative and uncertain elements in their life are typically more passive when they are confronted with difficulties. In this state of mind, they tend *not* to solve problems constructively, which then increases the possibility of anxiety and depression. They get used to doing what they have always done and don't challenge their thinking. They repeatedly do the things that keep them stuck.

Two things matter when you are molding your thoughts for the future: 1) the clear or muddy quality of the thought and 2) the shape of the container you put it in. If you go looking in your memory for positive experiences and emotions and find them, you remember what the experience was, and also what it felt like. The retrieval of the memory is shaped by the positive container used to retrieve it. By paying attention to what you want your thoughts to yield in the future, your choices create the shape of things to come.

Feel the Pull of Your Habits

Your mind will continually make the choices that you've made in the past. We are creatures of habit, but not only habits of behavior—habits of thought and feeling as well. Over time, patterns of thoughts, feelings, and behavior become the default response to a situation. If you've avoided challenges in the past and were passive in your response to them, avoidance would be your thought habit. If you then became anxious about the consequences, ruminated, and then became depressed—anxious and depressed would be your feeling habit. Good or bad, we get used to being in the world in a routine way. To change these habits requires deliberate effort. You must change your focus so that past choices don't become the default.

You can learn how automatic your habits are the next time you take a shower. Try using the opposite hand to brush your teeth, shampoo your hair, or wash your body. You'll see how challenging it is to go against the usual way of doing things. We normally don't even think about the routine—it's automatic. The sequence, temperature of the water, and physical routine of each task are barely conscious thoughts. By doing something different, you awaken your brain to the routine that is happening just under your awareness.

Thought habits operate under the radar most of the time too and are no less difficult to change. The good news is that once you have made the adjustments, they can become the new routine. The key is repetition. Whatever repeats endures.

Chronic negative, anxious, or depressing thoughts come from a habit of thinking. This tendency of thought shows up in a brain pattern that, as mentioned, is the default network. The brain's DN is a collective set of areas in the brain that kick in when we aren't specifically thinking about something or attending to a task.[66] In other words, when we are day-dreaming or not engaged with a specific external event, the DN is activated. While the research on the DN is still emerging, there are some interesting findings about how we worry—and what can be done about it.

Researchers who study the DN note that when people ruminate, they are "focused on their present mental and related autobiographical information rather than the future."[67] This is important information about how negative thinking keeps us stuck. Just like the routine in the shower is barely noticed—the DN keeps us unaware of the habit of thinking we are using. If we are ruminating in the moment, then the DN keeps us going in that loop.

Think of a toy train that keeps going in a circle even though there are other connected tracks it can take. Unless the railway switch moves the train off the track in a different direction, it will just keep going around and around. This is what happens during rumination. The DN puts us on a circular track, and we are likely to stay there until the railway switch changes our direction. If we are not looking for this switch, there is no chance we will flip it.

Confident people have learned how to find and flip that switch, because they are looking to do so. This empowers them to not get stuck going in circles. They have learned how to set that switch and deliberately take their thoughts into the future. They know how to break out of the DN. It all begins by first recognizing that the DN, the loop leading to nowhere, is happening. This is the essential first step in noticing that a change is needed.

For a moment, let's go back to thoughts being like water. Imagine you are getting your water from a stream. You grab a bucket and get water from the closest part of the stream—but the water from that section of the stream is stagnant and murky. You can taste it when you drink it. But the place you are getting it from is close by, so you keep getting it from that spot. It is the most available, so you keep going there.

When you recognize that you are getting the same unwanted results by doing the same thing—that is, when you are motivated to change—you will take deliberate action to go look for cleaner water. Once you realize that you are the one responsible for choosing that spot in the stream and returning to it—you are empowered to change.

With *deliberate effort* or *deliberate rumination*, you can replace the negative pattern with a new, positive one. You can direct these thoughts. They will then repeat—with some effort at first, because they are not as close and familiar as negative ones. If you don't steer them where you want them to go, they will take you back to where you've been. I invite you to explore how this works for yourself.

EXPLORATION: Yesterday and the Default Network

You will need to make a list—so please be sure to use your journal. Like all the exercises in this book, it will work best when you attend to it now, in the moment you encounter it. It builds on and enhances the material you've just been reading.

Think back to yesterday and make a list of everything you did. Take about one minute to do this. Here is one from a client of mine:

- Because I was anxious about the meeting, I got up early to prepare.

- Began sending out invoices and paying bills.

- I ordered batteries to be delivered because I was worried I wasn't going to have time to get to the store.

- Attended an online conference to hear the keynote.

- Took my vitamins.

- Saw a client, rescheduled two appointments, and ordered lunch to be delivered.

- Prepared for a presentation later in the day.

- Had technical problems during the presentation, but made it work.

- My partner came home, and we reviewed the day.

- Talked to my daughter and son-in-law about my granddaughter's first birthday.

- My partner and I went to the gym, then came home and had dinner.

- Watched some TV, then went to sleep a little earlier than usual.

What you may notice when you read through this list is the difference in language for function and emotion. Notice all the *functional* words in the example: *got up, sending, paying, ordered, took, prepared, reviewed, talked, watched*. And then the *emotional* words: *anxious, worried, problems*.

Now go through your list, the one created by your default network. Circle all of the functional words. Underline all of the emotional words.

Next, write about what you notice, and how this makes you feel about your day yesterday. Now, how would you respond to the question "How was your day yesterday?"

Chances are, you'll notice that it is the equivalent of your to-do list from yesterday—the things you checked off. There are not likely to be a cascade of positive feelings in the list. In fact, the feelings that break through—because they are so often the ones available—are the negative ones. Even when there could have been some positive emotions (*Talked to my daughter and son-in-law about my granddaughter's first birthday*), they weren't noted.

This list was retrieved using the DN. The DN chooses the answer it gives based on what it thinks the question is asking and the most-often-given answer. Just like when I typed in "how to cook fish" and the search engine pulled up what was available—the results were not optimal.

When we reflect in our typical way (before we learn how to activate the positivity effect), we get a generic response about what is in our minds. Like my Internet search, we won't necessarily get a helpful or the best answer, only the most common responses.

What can bring more positivity into your perspective? Just like when I specifically asked how to cook tuna on a barbecue—when you look for something specific, like a positive emotion, you will find much more of exactly what you need and want. When you ask the right questions, you get more helpful answers.

What Happens When You Recall with Gratitude

Let me start this section by speaking to the skeptical among you. When I first began learning about the power of positive emotions, combined with reducing negative ones, the research on gratitude was one of the first things I studied. It was interesting—even impressive—but no matter what research showed about the wonderful things that would happen when counting my blessings, I could not appreciate how such a small and innocuous thing could have all of these positive results. In spite of the fact that research has shown that gratitude has a broad and strong support on well-being,[68] it seemed too easy, too simplistic, too incidental—and I didn't try any of the exercises. I knew the research but didn't apply it.

Then my best friend, Joel, a positive psychologist as well, reminded me that knowing about gratitude isn't the same as understanding it. I began a daily gratitude practice that involves identifying, savoring, and becoming more aware of all the things I can be grateful for. If you get nothing else from *The Positivity Effect*, please know that having more gratitude in your life is the best place to start. It is the most likely practice to improve your well-being if done properly,[69] and has value and power as a positive emotion.[70] The reason a gratitude practice is so strong and an easy place to begin is threefold.

First, gratitude is most available because it is *always* about a past positive experience. Even if you give thanks to someone holding open a door, your gratitude follows the act. When these opportunities are missed and not capitalized on, the good things that have already happened need to be revisited, recalled, highlighted, and gathered for acknowledgment. *To change your future, change how you view the past.*

Second, you express gratitude when something or someone has acted on behalf of your well-being. It requires your empathy and altruism, which results in a thought–action sequence. This means, when you express gratitude, you have enjoyed benefits that have led to happiness. Your gratitude expands your ability to recognize good gifts and intentions—which then allows for the expression of more gratitude. This has been referred to as the *adaptive cycle of gratitude and happiness.* Specifically, gratitude promotes happiness, which in turn promotes more gratitude.[71] With apologies to Joe Raposo's song,[72] the research shows that if you're happy and you know it, putting your hands together and giving thanks starts an upward spiral of looking for more opportunities to repeat the process.

Finally, being thankful for what has made us happy increases prosocial behavior toward ourselves, others, or both. When you are grateful, you are likely to creatively consider a wide range of prosocial actions to reflect your gratitude. We are motivated to be kind and expand our positive actions toward others when we have gratitude.

In these three ways, gratitude, more than other forms of positivity, is in a unique position to transform how our default network scans for information.

EXPLORATION: Try On a Gratitude Lens

Now that you know what a gratitude lens does for positivity, review the previous day again. This time, make a list of at least three things that happened yesterday that you feel grateful about. This example list is from the same client as the previous list, in the same session.

- My presentation went much better than I planned, as I handled the technical error with ease and people had a very good response. I am very glad I didn't lose my cool.

- My friend called to let me know the tickets we had for a new show on Broadway was written by a playwright that I went to school with and she had made arrangements for us to meet after the show. I was ecstatic!

- It made me so happy to see my granddaughter on her birthday via FaceTime.

- I ordered dinner from my favorite Chinese food restaurant, and the egg rolls were even better than usual.

- My lunch was free because the service I use has a loyalty program. It was a nice perk in the middle of the day.

- At the gym, I met some new people in our building and it was very enjoyable.

- My partner and I snuggled together on the couch and fell asleep watching TV. It was the loveliest downtime we had all week.

Now, look at this second list and note the language. It isn't just functional—it uses a *positive* tone to describe the experience: *much better than I planned, a very good response, very glad, ecstatic, happy to see, even better than usual, a nice perk, loveliest.*

Look at your own list. Circle all the words or phrases that have a positive tone. What changed is the lens through which you viewed the day. This is important, as language is the container for positive emotions.

Now consider your two lists. Did all the positive items on the second list show up on the first list? Most likely not. Note that in the example, the memory of the call about the playwright wasn't even included in the first list. All that joy and gratitude was forgotten: unharvested and untapped. The default network will miss important things if gratitude isn't part of the algorithm for the search.

The second list shows the power of choosing the thoughts you are looking for. As you will recall, confident people pay attention to certain elements in their life. This is how they do it. They learn to look at things in a way that highlights experiences in their favor.

Of course, there is a balance to this. Truly confident people do not ignore the realities of a situation, but rather authentically let the positive outweigh the negative, through the use of this perspective. They see possibilities in the face of problems—not dismissing the difficulties. This naturally sets the stage for them to think about the future as full of potential and hope.

What You Choose to Recall Is the Secret of Confidence

Confident people feel empowered, and not worried, because they know how to search through their memories. They are selective about what they recall. The empowerment comes from knowing they control the choices they make—they choose to focus attention on their strengths, skills, and abilities. Instead of circling the endless track of worrying, they think about past successes, positive experiences, and good outcomes. Through selective memory retrieval, they also recollect and reactivate the positive feeling associated with the memory—bringing the dormant positive emotion to the present.

This is the secret to confidence. By focusing on what you choose to remember about the past, you can harvest the positive emotion from the memory and bring it into the moment. This positive state of readiness will move you forward into the future with a confidence that can help achieve your goals.

When you go looking for positive experiences and emotions and find them, don't stop at recalling what the experience was—also recall what it felt like. This is what flips the switch from a negative to a positive track. You get off the routine loop that doesn't yield much positivity; instead, you can go on your adventure with conviction and self-assurance. You can choose your memories, which determines the amount of positivity you experience.

Let's experiment further with a new way to search and retrieve positive information.

There Is Another Way to Look at This

If you recall, earlier we noted how the *13* is seen as a number or the letter *B* depending on how it is grouped. This points to the idea that one image can simultaneously be viewed as something completely different, depending on your perspective. This is what we are after when looking at how confident people view the same condition. Consider the image below.

If you are standing on the left end, the image you are looking at is the number 6. But if you are standing on the right end, the same image would be seen as 9. Both individuals standing at opposite ends would argue truthfully and accurately for what they were looking at. The key here is to understand that the perspective you have of something, although it seems absolute and without doubt, can be seen very differently.

To make this point a bit more dramatic, people who worry, are chronically anxious, and often depressed see a 6. Confident people look at the same situation in a different way and see the 9, because they have learned to search for another point of view. The worried will see limited potential and the confident will see much more. If someone with a history of being confident comes upon a situation in which they are confronted with a 6, they feel empowered to start looking at the situation differently. They do this by beginning a search for another way to look at what is given. If you will, the 6 is like what you found when you answered *How was your day?* above, and the 9 is what you found when you did it the second time, with your gratitude list.

Let's look at a story from the 6 and 9 perspectives. Here is an example from one of my clients.

> *I have a new boss who is trying to assert her power and authority and establish herself. She is asking me for reviews and reports, and information about my division that is taking a lot of time and seems never ending. I get her one piece of information she needs in the timeline she wants it in, and then immediately, she asks for three more things. It is taking me away from my daily routines, which then suffer and cause me to feel stressed and worried on a regular basis.*

I then asked her to look at this perspective from a new angle. What about these tasks is she grateful for? What potential could she see coming from this? Are there positives mixed into this process that she can extract and bring to the forefront? This is what she wrote.

> *Some of the things she has asked about are things I was only marginally aware of, and in gathering the information for her, I realized elements of my own division that were vital for me to know that I would have missed. Since she is new, this process gives me a chance to develop an early relationship with her, let her know about the needs of my division, and begin developing a good working relationship.*

It has also caused me to be more assertive and speak up for myself. Some of the requests I had to say no to, or change the timeline about when she wanted them. I'm typically not good at that—so this gave me an opportunity to be both assertive and clear. In every instance, when I explained myself, she understood and we renegotiated. This made me feel like what I had to say had value and she respected me as a professional.

Finally, by reviewing the material she has asked for, I started thinking of some creative ways of going forward. By looking at the features of my program differently, it stimulated my creativity to make some better plans for the future.

Notice how the same situation can be seen as burdensome and negative only, or seen from another way, can yield positivity. Which way do you believe would instill more confidence?

EXPLORATION: Flip Your Perspective

Now do the same with a situation from your life. Write about it from the 6 perspective first. Then ask yourself the following questions to see it from the 9 point of view.

What about the situation are you grateful for?

What potential could you see coming from this?

Are there positives mixed into this process that you can extract and bring to the forefront?

Notice how you felt when you wrote about the situation from the 9 point of view. In your journal, write down what you noticed about your feelings. Did you feel more empowered and confident? Jot down what made this change happen. Then reflect on how you might apply this to other areas in your life.

Psychological Self-Care Helps You Accomplish Your Goals

When scientists study confidence and empowerment, they often use the term *self-efficacy*, which has been around for a long time.[73] Self-efficacy is understood as a person's perceived ability to bring about desired outcomes.[74] It is most often studied in academic arenas when it comes to performance and business contexts, where it is sometimes referred to as *entrepreneurial* self-efficacy.[75]

The belief that you can make something happen is one of the most intriguing areas of study in positive psychology. We admire those who have the power to get things done, make things happen, and do it in a way that conveys they are happy and resilient. They rarely wallow in negativity. They do not avoid the reality of a situation; instead, they confront its challenges.

What makes for a confident, self-efficacious person? Research reveals a surprising answer. *Self-care* is the magic formula. This might seem like a dull or trite conclusion, but those who know how to engage in self-care anchor themselves in a way that makes them more confident and resilient.[76] We will be looking into resilience in the next chapter, but for now, let's take a deeper dive into self-care, what it means, and how it works to boost confidence.

Why would it be that taking good care of ourselves has such value? Self-care seems to make sense, of course, particularly when taking care of our physical well-being. This is obvious when brushing our teeth, taking a shower, exercising, getting enough sleep, and eating right. We have the sense that investing in our bodies in these ways allows us to feel and perform better, and the better we are, the more we'll want to keep investing in ourselves.

Self-care of any kind is a primary way to engage in the reciprocity of good feelings. In other words, when we have even a small belief that we can accomplish something, this instills the hope I described in the last chapter. This positive feeling then gets added to when the belief we have about accomplishing something is realized. When an engagement pays off, we've entered the positivity effect loop. The loop is bidirectional. When our effort has an effect, the effect supports the effort.

Psychological self-care is believing that the activities we've chosen to enhance our well-being have value. We engage because there is a potential good feeling at the end. When the good feeling arrives, it strengthens the motivation to do what brought it about.

Meditation is an example of one form of psychological self-care that can give us insight into why emotional self-regulation, the ability to observe and reflect on one's emotions, has tremendous value. When we meditate, we are trying to regulate how we feel, through reflection. The very act of trying to observe a feeling changes it, because you become a witness to it, rather than just an experiencer of it. Different meditations achieve this in various ways. As a small sample, various types of meditations have been shown to reduce prejudice;[77] symptoms of mental illness;[78] physical pain;[79] post-traumatic stress disorder (PTSD);[80] the stress hormone cortisol;[81] stress, anxiety, depression, and rumination;[82] and the self-criticism underlying depression.[83] Other results show increases in self-compassion[84] as well as emotional reappraisal, well-being, and mindfulness.[85]

With meditation, you deliberately attend to your consciousness in a way that's different from your normal awareness. This deliberate way of attending to your thoughts begins the regulation process. The moment you knowingly begin to reflect on your thought, it changes the nature of what you are thinking about. This pause for thought is where the value is. When you decide to try meditation, you are doing so because you *believe* it may be helpful and worth a try. Feeling the impact of the results motivates you to keep investing in meditation. The loop is self-reinforcing, self-evident, and self-sustaining.

While I highly recommend meditation, let's start with something simpler. To gain confidence, you can begin by harvesting your everyday positive emotions. This is like collecting wood for a bonfire. Positive emotions are the fuel to warm up your life. Once ignited, they breed confidence. The loop that leads to empowerment and sustainable behavioral change can begin with this: shift your awareness from one way of seeing or experiencing the world to a different way. We discussed this in the last chapter with the *13* or *B*, and in this chapter with the *6* or *9*. By regulating your awareness to look for, generate, or appreciate the positivity around you, your perception adds more feathers for better balance in your life. When you can shift toward positive feelings, you will "open the mind and nourish the growth of resources."[86]

At the core of this is loving-kindness meditation. As the name might imply, it focuses on cultivating feelings of inclusive, non-romantic love, goodwill, kindness, and compassion. Although originating in the Buddhist tradition, it has enjoyed tremendous popularity because of the scientific findings showing an increase of positive emotions, a reduction of negative ones,[87] and improving social connections.[88, 89]

EXPLORATION: The Power to Change to Positivity

The simplest way to start gathering fuel for your confident, empowered self is to prove you can deliberately change how you feel. This is how to do psychological self-care by activating positive emotions. It draws on components from research on loving-kindness meditation.[90]

You will need your journal for this. Plan to do this three-part exercise all at once. As always, *please* do the exercise now, before you continue reading. This is the very essence of the work you came to do, and it will give you the emotional experience that begins the upward spiral and reciprocity you are looking for.

Part 1

1. Make three columns in your journal: *BODY, THOUGHTS,* and *FEELINGS*. Begin by writing down exactly how you are experiencing these things, at this moment.

2. Start by tuning into your body. Scan your body for sensations, focusing on each area, from your toes to your head. What are you sensing in your shoulders, neck, stomach, legs? What are you most aware of? Where do you feel things? Be as descriptive as you can be about these sensations in the *BODY* column.

3. Move on to noticing your thoughts. What are the words you are using to think? What are your concerns? Are they about the past? The future? Is there a connection between what your body is feeling and your thoughts? Write your observations in the THOUGHTS column.

4. Turn your attention to your feelings. What emotions are you having as you do this exercise? Is there a connection between your body, thoughts, and feelings? Write down what you notice in the FEELINGS column.

Part 2

1. Shake out your hands and legs, then rotate your head in one direction, then another. Take three deep breaths. Then turn to a new page in your journal and again make three columns for BODY, THOUGHTS, and FEELINGS.

2. This time, think about someone difficult for you. A person who has caused you grief, upset, or disappointment. Write their name at the top of the page.

3. As you recall this person, tune into your body. Scan your body, from toe to head, and focus on each area. What are you sensing in your shoulders, neck, stomach, legs now? What are you most aware of? Where do you feel things? Record the sensations you have while thinking about this difficult person in the BODY column.

4. Move on to writing down your thoughts about this person. What are the words you are using to think? What are your concerns? Are they about past experiences with this person? Future experiences with this person? Is there a connection between what your body is feeling and your thoughts? Note them in the THOUGHTS column.

5. Now write down how recalling this person makes you feel. What emotions are you having as you picture them? Write down what you notice in the *FEELINGS* column.

6. Observe whether there is a connection between the descriptions in the three columns. What is it? What do you notice about how recalling this difficult person affects you?

Stop and compare what you wrote down for Parts 1 and 2. What changed? Where were the changes most noticeable? In your body? Thoughts? Feelings?

Now let's explore the positivity effect.

Part 3

For Part 3, on a left-hand page in your journal, make three columns of people: 1) whom you love and who love you; 2) whom you like and who like you; and 3) whom you enjoy being around and who enjoy being around you. One person should be on any of those lists only once; each list should be a unique group of people.

Then look at the list and pull up a scene in your mind, a moment when you felt the positivity between you and anyone whose name you wrote down. This is referred to as *positivity resonance*.[91]

1. Shake out your hands and legs, then rotate your head in one direction, then another. Take three deep breaths. Then start a new page in your journal and make three columns: *BODY, THOUGHTS,* and *FEELINGS*.

2. Recall the scene with the person and hold on to this feeling. Notice what happens in your body. Write about these sensations in the *BODY* column.

3. Now write down your thoughts as you hold each person in your mind's eye. What do you notice about your thinking? Are there now connections between your thoughts and your body? Write your observations in the *THOUGHTS* column.

4. In the *FEELINGS* column, record what it feels like as you recall these memories. What emotions do you experience? How do these feelings show up in your thoughts and body? Are there any connections you can notice?

Wrap up by comparing the three lists—how you felt: initially; when you thought of a negative person; and then during the positivity resonance exercise. Answer the following questions in your journal.

- What changed? What bodily sensations, thoughts, and emotions shifted as you recalled the positive people on your list?

- Do you think this had a benefit for you? Specifically, did the recall of people you have positivity resonance with change your feelings, thoughts, and body positively?

- How might you use this experience of shifting your focus during your day-to-day life?

You changed your feelings in just a few moments—through the power of thought. When you think about someone positively, you have positivity resonance with your thoughts, body, and feelings. Your experience changes instantaneously. You've just proven to yourself that you can change what you are feeling by shifting your attention.

These explorations together show the power of relationships—good and bad. We began with where you were, in the moment. You could sway your thoughts in a negative direction by thinking about the person who gave you grief. Then we switched to the accumulated loving and positive experiences we hold in our memories, and our capacity to activate them whenever we need them. Depending on whom you thought of—the negative person or the positive—your body, thoughts, and feelings changed.

I invited you to recall one and then the other in this exercise, but this ability is yours to use at your discretion. Whenever your mind has been hijacked by negative ruminating thoughts and worry, you can deliberately think of the people with whom you have positivity resonance. This is psychological self-care through emotional self-regulation.

EXPLORATION: Act to Invite More of What You Want

Now let's focus on the power of positivity resonance and prosocial behavior.[92] You can cultivate what is already good by amplifying, celebrating, and honoring the relationships in your life. You have the power to change how you are thinking and actively change what you are doing.

1. Starting today, begin making brief contact with one person you listed as a positive connection. Start right now. Send a text or an email, give a call, use social media, send a card, visit, etc. Record in your journal what this experience is like for you.

2. Continue doing this once a day until you've connected with everyone on the list. At the end of the experiences, reflect on the process and the feelings it generated.

3. After you do this for a while, notice which you appreciate more: thinking about someone (as you did in the previous exercise) or acting to reach out to them? Which was more effective in generating positive emotions? What are the ripple effects of each one? Of them combined?

I want you to know that you can use both of these exercises at any time to change how you feel. They use the strongest form of positivity, our relationships, to make this shift. By allowing yourself to make a deliberate change in how you feel, you demonstrate the ability for self-care. This simple act gives you the power to make things happen. It is the birthplace of confidence and empowerment.

Now let's take this a step further. Each moment you see positively builds on the previous one and leads to another. This can have a profound effect on your life.

I Believe, Therefore I Achieve (and Vice Versa)

In business, school, and relationships, the confident among us have mastered a profound principle of success. They have uncovered and live by a truism: Thoughts shape who you are, and their quality determines your success. In other words: *Believing something is possible is the best way to achieve it.*

I am sure you've heard this idea before. Positive thinking has been around for a very long time. Yet there is a second half to this proverbial wisdom for confident people: *Achieving what I believe strengthens my confidence.*

Confident people know there is a loop, a reciprocity of dynamics.[93] To make something achievable, you must believe it is possible. Once it has happened, this supports the feeling that it can be done again. For the confident, there is continuity that says: *Achieving something I believed possible strengthens my confidence.*

When you are not in a confident space, you can still make this reciprocity work. You can believe that some smaller goal can be accomplished, see this get achieved, and then feel the positive feedback—which fuels more belief for the next time, perhaps for an effort that is a bit bigger. By scaffolding in this way, you can be empowered by your successes. You start to see yourself as an agent of change, where positive emotions are fueled by beliefs. This leads to creative coping strategies and improves your positivity.

Confident people engage in what Barbara Fredrickson has called an *upward spiral of lifestyle change*.[94] This upward spiral is available to all of us. It begins with smaller goals and works its way up. The principle remains the same whether we are fully confident or just beginning. Just a bit of belief that you can accomplish something—anything—will initiate this upward spiral.

The dynamics of this spiral are based on Dr. Fredrickson's *broaden and build* theory. It demonstrates that regular, mild, everyday positive emotions change our awareness. Which, as Dr. Fredrickson puts it, "open the mind and nourish the growth of resources."[95]

You now know how to choose positivity. Doing this repeatedly gives momentum to the positivity effect.

Now that you've seen how the confident get that way, let's turn our attention to how they stay resilient. We'll explore how, when you experience hardship, you can bounce forward instead of falling back.

CHAPTER 4

RESILIENCE: Gain Courage Amidst Challenges with a Flexible Mindset

The impediment to action advances action. What stands in the way becomes the way.

—Marcus Aurelius

Have you ever planned how something would go, only to find your expectations derailed? A person you believed in or counted on let you down. A situation you thought was assured didn't come to pass. Or an accomplishment you thought would fill you up didn't. Whenever we don't get the results we want, disappointment sets in, and we are left to cope.

Yet this is just part of being human. To believe things should go one way and then have them go in another direction is central to our being. As John Lennon sang: "Life is what happens when you're busy making other plans."

When things don't go our way, we can be resilient or fragile, ready or unprepared, resourceful or overextended. Research has explored what makes people cope in various ways. Of course, sometimes we get lovely surprises, when the expected didn't come to pass but things turned out better than what we could have hoped. For example: the hotel lost your reservation and offered an upgrade as an apology. But when life's unexpected twists and turns happen, we usually experience them negatively.

This chapter is about finding resilience when your assumptions are interrupted by a setback. We'll focus on what happens when the unexpected turns negative, and what you can do about it. Then, in the next chapter on optimism, I will show you how the good and not-so-good surprises together can allow you to cultivate a high degree of readiness and preparedness for life.

Perceiving Adversity as a Threat or a Challenge

Researchers understand resilience in two ways: It can mean the capacity to resist being impacted by setbacks or destructive experiences. It can also refer to our psychological ability to bounce back after these experiences.[96] The first definition refers to how people survive, the second to how they thrive. When we face adversity, we have the potential to do more than merely cope. Our attitude toward the conflict is the key ingredient in the outcome. How we view the situation determines how we respond.

If we greet a situation as a threat—it becomes one. This is when our choices for dealing with it become limited. When facing a threat, we react with limited responses. We must resist our human tendency to appraise a situation only as dangerous and threatening. This is another way the negativity bias works, because worrying has adaptive value—in human history, we survived when we worried.[97] But if we want to thrive, we must keep this tendency in perspective. If we don't put the negativity bias in check, it will limit our options for response. We'll be left ruminating as we frantically search for solutions we don't have, in a state of chronic worry.

When we assess the same situation with an open attitude, from multiple angles and different perspectives, it becomes a challenge. A perceived challenge brings more available options to the situation than a perceived threat. With challenges, we use more resources proactively. Whether we perceive the situation as a threat or a challenge will determine how we cope with adversity.

When a problematic situation arises, we can learn to use the difficulty to reassess and reexamine our thoughts. This is what people who have resilience do. This reappraisal—known by psychologists as *cognitive reappraisal*—can help us find meaning in difficulty. We use this new way of looking at things, this shift in perspective that brings meaning, to improve our well-being. It is what can help us not only bounce back—but bounce forward.[98] Let's explore how the nature of our minds makes this resilience possible.

The Mind's Response to Obstacles

Scientists who study how our brain and mind work have determined that humans make mental representations of possible futures in a process called *prospection*. This usually serves to move us forward in a positive way.[99] We think about what we want in the future, plan how to achieve it, and execute these plans. It is typically adaptive and successful. From the moment we wake up in the morning and make the plan to get out of bed, brush our teeth, and get dressed, our mind is engaged in prospection. It's asking: *What do I want? What do I need to do to get it? What is the most efficient way for this happen?* This is, by and large, how we think. We live in the future—imagining what's to come.

Your mind is prospective by nature, one of the most potent assets of being human.[100] You can imagine future possibilities, potentialities, and pitfalls. You don't just imagine what is already there—you generate and evaluate alternative possibilities.[101] This is perhaps the most dynamic and constructive nature of your consciousness.

Think of your mind as a forecasting machine making assessments and predictions. When you get these predictions right, all is well with you. You feel aligned, make your way successfully, and have some sense of positivity about the accomplishment. The good feeling comes from the successful adaptive strategy that helped you achieve your goal. You planned your morning routine to get to work on time, prepared an excellent dinner enjoyed by all, wrote a paper for class, got it in on time, and received a good grade. A good feeling follows successful prospection.

That's what happens when things are working well. But something else happens when the situation goes awry. With a negativity bias, the future is something to worry about. It triggers a worry signal. The negativity bias becomes a threat appraisal. If you follow the same route to work, school, or the store each day and there is an unexpected detour, it throws you off because your intention was disrupted. When there is an obstacle to your plan for the future, it becomes problematic for the future-forecasting machine. Your mind decides if it is being threatened or challenged, and it must reexamine and reappraise what to do in response. More often than not, because of how we were designed, we make the appraisal that there is something to worry about. This starts an avalanche of concern.

Here's an everyday example: you get up, put on your slippers, go to the bathroom, wash your hands, and get ready to brush your teeth. But when you look for the toothpaste, it's gone—the expectation and the situation don't align. Having no toothpaste is a small thing, but it disrupts the expectation and creates a moment of choice. What are you going to do? There are many options for what to do in this situation. It's so minor, but the responses are vast. Here are a few.

- This could be yet another time your partner has finished the toothpaste and didn't replace it. You might be upset about this and decide you need to speak to them about it so it doesn't happen again.

- You might recall that you finished it and forgot to buy more—and begin searching for a spare in the medicine cabinet.

- You might not believe it is gone, as it was there and full yesterday—so you might check the shower or see if it may have fallen.

- You could look for substitutes and see if there is any baking soda or decide to brush your teeth without toothpaste.

- You might borrow some from another bathroom.

An obstacle initiates action. Yet to initiate that action, the barrier must first cause a reappraisal. Your brain considers innumerable options in fractions of a second. Notice that with each option, the direction of the action differs, depending on your assessment of what's happening—and what you can do about it. Do you get angry at your partner, or realize you finished the toothpaste yesterday? Do you not concern yourself with what happened, but just go looking for a replacement? Do you take a swig of mouthwash and move on with your day like nothing happened?

Fueled by thoughts, our belief about the situation sparks and initiates a direction for action. This is where the obstruction—whatever stops us from continuing on our prospective path—offers a mental space to work out a new approach. This *pause for thought* is where all the power resides and when the positivity effect can enter the process and begin to inform the direction and decision.[102]

Options Beyond the Negativity Bias

If you have ever missed a turn while following your GPS (Global Positioning System), you may have noticed a brief moment where the unit tells you that it is "rerouting." A path forward hasn't emerged just yet. It is considering how to guide your next move. The course forward is being charted, but at that moment, the exact path hasn't been identified. The GPS unit is reexamining, reappraising, and rerouting to find new ways to get you to your destination.

This is the same as what happens when your thoughts about the action to be taken are in deep prospection about possibilities and options. Your prospection thoughts are like a GPS unit recalculating. You still want to achieve your goal but must find a different way to get there. Here are some rerouting tips that bypass the negativity bias.

Pause to Think

When we pause for thought, we can grasp for interpretations and alternatives. Taking even a brief moment to allow this pause can give us time to resist the urge to interpret a situation only as a threat. Instead, we can experiment with new options, alternatives, and possibilities.

Extending this pause for thought is a gift you can give yourself. When what you were planning hasn't worked, you need time to think.[103]

Luckily, since your brain works so quickly, deliberately giving yourself just the slightest moment allows various perspectives and options to come into play. The GPS unit is slow and clunky compared to your brain's speed and sophistication. You are prospective as you think about the future and make plans to achieve your goals. At the moment you get thrown off your expectations—even if just because of a small thing—there is a precious instant when you decide what action to take. The forecasting machine has to recalculate—just like your GPS must do when your route is blocked. When you come to a detour you didn't foresee, take the time to reexamine, reappraise, and recalculate how to get to your destination.

Recall When You Successfully Navigated Setbacks Before

I once tried to drive to Boston, a city that had gone through tremendous replanning and reconstruction, with an outdated map. Because I hadn't updated the GPS, the map was no help at all. I remember distinctly being at a stoplight, and the unit said, "Take a right at the light." The map clearly showed a street that headed due east, but I saw a massive multistory parking garage instead.

If the history of our choices (our old maps) has been filled with options that might have worked once but are no longer viable, they can lead to dead ends, negativity, and poor outcomes. This means that when we grasp for thoughts about the current hindrance, we don't get the best options, because we are basing conclusions on a negative past history. Our options aren't aligned with adequate solutions, decent alternatives, or successful outcomes. When the prospects for our choices are outdated and inaccurate, actions taken can be dissatisfying, limiting, and can lead to the beginning of a downward spiral.

To change the kind of action we choose, we need to stay refreshed and updated by learning new information—otherwise, we might end up in a multistory parking garage. Similarly, we can improve our own accuracy by ensuring we have the most up-to-date information and options available. Just like my GPS unit needed an upgrade, our options need to be updated in order for us to become more resilient. Pay attention to more-recent data, especially from the present moment—which is not biased by past negative information.

Check In with the Moment for Options

What maps are you using to get to your destination? If you are stuck, lost, blocked, or set back, could it be that your directions are outdated? Significantly, the choices we make as we grasp for answers depend on the options we tell ourselves are available. When it comes to navigating a challenge, be open to considering a variety of successful, efficient, and effective course corrections. This is the equivalent of adding a real-time traffic report to updated maps. By considering specific information about which path is the best at the moment, your thinking can generate alternatives on demand—depending on the circumstances. When you update your inner GPS and check in with what is happening at the moment, you'll be better prepared to get around obstacles.

Researchers tell us that our capacity for dealing with setbacks has to do with two essential features: how well we have dealt with various setbacks in the past, and the adaptability of our thinking—or what is known as *flexible self-regulation*.[104] To not just bounce back, but bounce forward, we want to have experiences that show we have figured out how to get through situations, and the agility to think through multiple pathways to reach a goal.

Recovering Your Balance through Awareness

In this chapter, so far I chose a small obstacle (losing toothpaste) as an example, to show how our mind responds. When we get to more significant issues, like divorce, betrayals, and trauma, our deeply emotional nature can overshadow our efforts at clarity.

Say your expectation in a critical situation was interrupted, disrupted, or stopped. You hoped to stay in your job, get married, go on vacation, have a second child, retire early, lose weight, make the plane on time, be promoted, or not yell at your children. In these moments, you may have the feeling of shutting down, of not being able to figure out what to do or how to move forward.

This confusion is typical. When we have a shattered assumption about a situation, the unmet expectation throws us off-kilter.[105]

But we are built to be in balance, so when we are not, our whole system strives to get us back. Think of a time when you were physically thrown off-balance—slipping on a patch of ice while walking, misjudging a step, or perhaps tripping on the foyer rug. What happens? You immediately scramble to get yourself back into balance. The brain and body work together to get you back into a balanced state. You instantly redistribute your weight, possibly swinging your legs wide and planting your feet in ways very different from how they were moving. Perhaps you take several quick steps to keep from falling. Your arms swing out to help secure stability. And you do all this quickly. This is the physical equivalent of resilience. You don't just bounce back—you bounce forward, as a reaction to the obstacle.

Whether we can't find the toothpaste or we lose our job, there is one thing we know is happening—we are thrown off. When we get thrown off-balance emotionally, psychologists call this *disequilibrium.* When we are stable, in harmony, and aligned, this is *equilibrium*—a natural, preferred state. The critical awareness behind how the change happens is that we know when we feel not okay, not ourselves. We know our balanced state is missing, which starts a chain reaction to strive to return to it. There's a big difference between feeling okay, and not.

Inside us, there is an inner observer-self that monitors how we feel and whether we are okay or not. I don't think it matters much whether we call this aspect of ourselves the *self, observing self,* or *observing ego.* Some call it a *higher self*—because it is neither balanced nor imbalanced but looks at both from a "higher" perspective. A spiritual view might refer to this observer as a *higher power, transcendent self, soul,* or as Deepak Chopra has identified it, the *nonlocal self.*[106] Whatever the term, the function of this aspect of our awareness is to experience ourselves and note whether or not we are balanced. This is the part of us that is responsible for self-regulation. Like a tightrope walker or someone walking across a ship at sea, we are constantly ensuring that we are adequately poised. This observing/higher/nonlocal self makes tiny adjustments along the way, and big ones when necessary.

Our brains have this excellent observer capacity. It's a large part of what makes us human. It is this awareness that we are striving to expand when we cultivate resilience, because once we are aware of disequilibrium, we can deliberately create an opportunity for a mindful pause, to recalculate and engage prospection.

Once we acknowledge the discomfort imbalance brings, we become aware that we are not in our aligned state. We want to do everything we can to get our equilibrium back. Psychologists broadly categorize the actions we take to manage this obstacle as *self-regulation*. The disruption of our well-being activates a need for correction.

Scientists have known for a long time that disequilibrium is an initiator and integrator of equilibrium, and that disequilibrium initiates self-regulation of emotions.[107] When we are off, the observing part of us knows it. Disequilibrium promotes equilibrium. Being off-balance causes us to strive for stability. Awareness of the need to regulate is followed by a sense of agency: that the discomfort can be reduced and transformed.

We want to regain control. When we are physically thrown off, our reactions are meant to keep us from falling. When we are emotionally thrown off, self-regulation uses our awareness to choose the best options. All this is to say: What stands in the way (disequilibrium) *becomes* the way (to strive for balance/equilibrium). We are wired to recover from hardship.

Getting Up after a Fall

Resilience is about facing adversity and thriving. As a recap, here's how it works. Our mind works in prospection—thinking about future possibilities—and this thinking forms plans to achieve goals. When these plans and expectations run into obstacles, a moment emerges when we can reexamine, reappraise, and recalculate—just like our GPS. It is the moment we are aware that we must decide how to respond. When that response is proactive and accepting of the situation as a challenge, we move toward it with conviction. There is something we can do to change it. When we are blocked from our expectations, the disequilibrium initiates equilibrium through self-regulation. Our awareness allows for reappraisal, and for new choices to be made for action.

This we know from scientific research about people who have been resilient after a difficulty befalls them. But what makes them *want* to get up? Some do this naturally. Dr. George Bonanno, a leading researcher on resilience, has long promoted the position that people are much more robust, more resilient, and less fragile than we think. He defines resilience as *"the ability of individuals exposed to a potentially highly disruptive event to maintain both healthy psychological and physical functioning and the capacity for positive emotions."*[108] He profoundly understands what makes for resilience and has determined that the research can't predict who will be resilient. Resilience research typically shows correlation *after* the trauma, meaning we know who *became* resilient following a potentially traumatic event. However, this doesn't translate into understanding who will be resilient at an individual level when a disruptive event happens. This is known as the *resilience paradox*.[109] The result is that scientists focus less on who *will become* resilient and more on who *has*.

This is good news, because it means there isn't a resilient type—someone who has stress-coping ability versus someone who doesn't. There's no particular personality that is or isn't resilient. After all, no key traits are beneficial in every situation or point in time. Instead, the mechanism underlying resilience is the capacity to appraise and assess the best option for moving forward, on a moment-to-moment basis. Resilient people can use the disequilibrium and the moment of reassessment and recalculation to consider possibilities and opportunities—and then engage in them. When they get off-balance, they are primed to thrive, not just survive. According to Bonanno, these people have learned self-regulation via a *flexible mindset*.[110]

A flexible mindset develops when you can reflect on the answers to four essential questions during a difficult time:

- What is happening?

- What do I need to do?

- What am I able to do?

- Is it working?[111]

Because you have an observer awareness as part of your human consciousness, you can learn to pause for thought, as resilient people do when a crisis is upon them. This moment is when—and where—flexible thinking can be advanced. The ongoing assessment is where the flexibility is nurtured. If the action chosen is working, then it becomes monitored. If not, then the mind begins cycling through the questions again.

How to Develop a Flexible Mindset

Like when we take a yoga class or do stretching exercises to develop our physical flexibility, there are ways to build a flexible mind. If you have ever woken up achy and felt the need to stretch (and who hasn't?), the discomfort prompts the need for relief through more flexibility. Once we see some relief, we may begin stretching as a regular part of our routine to prevent, not just cope with, the aches and pains. This is also true with emotional well-being.

The need for a flexible mindset is initially brought on by discomfort—or what we now know is disequilibrium. We need to stretch our minds when faced with an achy situation. Then, we learn to stretch to avoid aches. We improve our resilience in disruptive situations by developing the ability to be flexible. This is what resilient people do—and you can learn to do it more.

Let's go back to the toothpaste example. The disruption in the expectation—"Where's the toothpaste?"—creates a moment for appraisal and action, and the first two questions become front and center in our mind: "What is happening?" and then, "What do I need to do?" Research focuses on this initial moment as the time and place to use the first step in flexibility. It *requires* reflection. That observing part of us must try and understand what is happening—and what can be done. This is where the brain shifts gears—if it is ready, and if it is flexible enough to do so.

But what if we are not ready? At this first step, if we do not have a flexible mindset and reflect on the situation, we will experience defeatism.[112] This is when our beliefs about a situation are that any effort is futile because nothing could change the outcome. Events that involve loss, rejection, and failure are significant, but being blocked or frustrated on the way toward any goal can activate this feeling. Whenever we feel we cannot have an impact on our future, the hopelessness often leads to defeatist coping. This is when we use denial, alcohol, drugs, self-criticism, excessive sleep, and giving up as ways to deal.[113] Or, more precisely—to not deal.

To improve our coping, at this first step we must resist defeatism and instead pause for thought. This is what the resilient among us do. It is the way to prevent a defeatist reaction and create enough opportunity for emotional regulation. The pause is regulation, in and of itself. If we pause to consider the situation, we are already self-regulating. A pause is progress. It gives us the best chance to answer the four essential questions with positivity rather than negativity.

When we can no longer continue on a chosen or desired path, we need a new solution. But this solution requires a moment to come about. This ability to shift gears is our initial capacity to tune into and reflect on our emotional and physiological state following a setback. Being able to do this accurately allows for choosing the best or most appropriate ways of responding to difficulty. Following a psychological disruption, awareness of what is happening and what can be done may be resilient people's most important skill set. It can answer the first two questions—*What is happening?* and *What do I need to do?*—with less influence from the negativity bias. The pause prevents us from being flooded with worry, and therefore gives us more and better options to choose from as we reexamine, reappraise, and reroute.

The resilient resist defeatism by not letting it start. If you can bring a higher degree of accuracy in assessing your emotional and psychological state by first pausing, you will be more capable of self-regulation. The less negativity you allow, the greater the opportunity for positivity.[114]

The pause for thought might sound obvious or trivial, but it is essential for creating a space where a threat appraisal can be challenged, alternatives considered, and options for action allowed. The pause can transform reactions into responses, defeatism into choices, and avoidance into readiness. Only then can you explore the alternatives for action and assessment with the questions *What am I able to do?* and *Is it working?*

Taking stock in the present moment is nothing new, but learning to cultivate this trait has become the subject of great interest and research.[115] *Dispositional mindfulness* harvests understanding and insight into what is happening at the moment. This pause has long been seen as the central skill in detaching and unhooking from *automatic negative thoughts* (known as *ANTS*) and unhealthy or destructive behaviors while promoting self-regulation.[116] This is the very seed of resilience.

EXPLORATION: Cultivating Mindfulness-Awareness in Any Moment

This exploration will come in two parts. The first is developing a mindful awareness of any given moment so that you begin cultivating the capacity to pause for thought. The second part will be learning how to, more specifically, foster an awareness of what strength you are using in that moment. First, you'll learn how to pause and reflect. Then you'll learn how to identify your strength.

Please mark the date and time in your journal, then read through these three steps. Take a moment to practice them and record your reactions in your journal.

1. Whatever you are doing, pause the activity and focus your attention on your breath. Don't try to speed up your breath or slow it down. Just become aware of it. Feel your in-breath and out-breath for 10 seconds. This is the pause.

2. Ask yourself: What am I feeling, physically and emotionally? There is no right or wrong to this. You are not trying to make anything happen. Instead, you are expanding awareness by pausing to notice what is already there, good or bad. Here's my list in the current moment: excited, comfortable, hopeful, creative, rested.

3. Reflect on what it means for you to become aware of your experience in this moment.

The value of this pause is that it allows you to become aware that while your attention may be focused on one aspect of a moment, other features are coexisting and available for review if you pause to notice them.

Several valuable features come with this practice. First, it helps keep you in touch with your reactions by having you connect to your experience. Second, it cultivates the observing, higher, or nonlocal self, which gives you perspective on the moment that you might not otherwise have. Finally, this pause offers an expanded opportunity to answer the essential questions *What is happening? What do I need to do? What am I able to do?* and *Is it working?*[117] To contemplate these questions, developing a pause for thought facilitates a state of preparedness. Just like when beginning an exercise program, yoga, or meditation practice, you want to cultivate your awareness.

I recommend that you repeat this pause three times a day, to get in the habit of checking in with yourself, no matter what you are doing—just a brief assessment to expand awareness. Doing so will make you ready for resilience by assessing the situation, options, possibilities, and whether what you've chosen to do is effective.

As we go up against a potentially defeatist attitude, we can use the pause for reflection as the beginning of self-regulation, and to understand what other tools might be available to us at the moment. We are expanding the *inner grasp,* our incipient moment where we search for an answer about how to respond. This expands what resources we have available to us while simultaneously limiting the negativity that can come pouring in.

Now let's look at part two of this exercise as a way to enhance the ability to act beneficially, in the midst of a challenging moment, as we consider our available strengths.

Infusing the Pause with Your Strengths

Not reacting with defeatism is the first step in choosing how to readily respond with alternatives. The second step to cultivating a flexible mindset is looking at your obstacle, or challenge, through the lens of your character strengths.[118] Character strengths are widely regarded as significant contributions to the field of positive psychology and offer ways to identify non-intellectual factors that can profoundly affect our well-being. You can learn more about them at the website viacharacter.org.[119]

In my previous book, *Learned Hopefulness*,[120] I wrote about the value of character strengths in depth. For our purpose, a brief review follows. The following is a list of character virtues, and the strengths associated with them. This collection was developed after exhaustive research.[121]

1. *Wisdom and Knowledge: creativity or innovation, curiosity, open-mindedness, love of learning, perspective*

2. *Courage: bravery, persistence, integrity, vitality, zest*

3. *Humanity: love, kindness, social intelligence*

4. *Justice: citizenship, fairness, leadership*

5. *Temperance: forgiveness and mercy, humility, prudence, self-control*

6. *Transcendence: appreciation of beauty and excellence, gratitude, hope, humor, spirituality*

These virtues/strengths are quickly becoming the core new wave of investigation and practice in psychology. To date, over 30 million people in two hundred countries have taken an online character strength survey. The tool is so powerful precisely because it was developed based on virtues and character traits valued around the world and across all known cultures. A summary description from the VIA website indicates, "Most personality tests focus on negative and neutral traits, but the VIA Survey focuses on your best qualities."[122]

Research shows that by focusing on your best qualities—your character strengths—in a moment of challenge, you can significantly improve your well-being, capacity to thrive, and ability to engage.[123] This is a direct way to move toward more positivity, confidence, and resilience. We are better prepared when we know what character strength tools are at our disposal.

Consider the following list of strengths. Think about which of these strengths are with you right now. My list in this instant, as I write, would include creativity, curiosity, love of learning, zest, appreciation of excellence, hope, and self-regulation. What strengths are you experiencing in this moment, as you read this book?

- Creativity

- Curiosity

- Judgment

- Love of Learning

- Perspective

- Bravery

- Perseverance

- Honesty

- Zest

- Kindness

- Love

- Social Intelligence

- Teamwork

- Fairness

- Leadership

- Forgiveness

- Humility

- Prudence

- Appreciation of Beauty and Excellence

- Self-Regulation

- Gratitude

- Hope

- Humor

- Spirituality

Being in touch with the strengths we are using in the moment is a direct way of cultivating our thoughts and feelings. Below is a way we can extend this practice on a regular basis.

EXPLORATION: The Mindful Pause

A mindful pause was developed by Dr. Ryan Niemiec of the VIA Institute on Character. It is an exquisitely easy way to begin cultivating the capacity to pause as we tumble through our day.[124] As always, please allow yourself to do this exercise now, as it will help you understand the material and future explorations. It will also immediately give you a needed tool in developing resilience.

1. Mark the date and time in your journal. Pause to focus your attention on your breath. Don't try to speed it up or slow it down; just become aware of it. Feel your in-breath and out-breath for 10 seconds.

2. Check in with yourself and be curious about what you are feeling, physically and emotionally. Write down some observations.

3. Review the list of 24 character strengths and ask yourself which of them you are using right now—at this moment.

4. Reflect on what it means for you to become aware of these character strengths.

This brief exploration allows for a pause and reflection on your physical and emotional feelings, and then which of your character strengths are operating at the moment. When we pause, it gives us time to under-stand what is happening with our body and our feelings, initiates self-regulation, and allows us to assess our strengths. This expansion of awareness is deliberate and initially needs to be intentional, until you become proficient at pausing and reflecting regularly. Research shows that pausing, becoming mindful of the moment, and acknowledging our strengths are helpful tools in improving how we cope with stress and improve well-being and relationships.[125]

By keeping defeatism at bay and bringing more resources to the table, the pause helps us answer the first two questions, *What is happening?* and *What do I need to do?* As we move into answering *What am I able to do?* and *Is it working?*, we move from assessment to action. We get to test our thinking and capabilities. For this, we can look to those who have come before us—and whose resilience we admire.

Often the traits within us that we wish to develop are those we admire in other people. With resilience, as with the other factors of HERO, real people can be superb role models of what we aspire to become.

The traits and abilities that emerge in us cause us to notice them in others. Whenever we are looking to develop a quality, characteristic, skill, or attitude, the people who are already displaying these features tell us precisely what we need to build. By focusing specifically on a few of your role models, you may get a clearer picture of what you wish to become.

EXPLORATION: The Flexible Mindset of Resilient Role Models

Let's take this deeper, by looking at the people you identify as resilient. For this exercise, look for people who shine for you. We have been talking about general resilience features, but now it is time to get specific to your needs. As you focus on different elements of resilience displayed in dif-ferent individuals, you will see in others what you may need to develop in yourself.

For this exercise, pick three people you believe to be resilient, and note them in your journal. Choose them for the type of resilience you want to have more of in your life, and are drawn to.

For my examples, I chose James, a thought-leader who is constantly being alternately honored and attacked for his work; Michelle, a woman who, despite consistent physical problems, disciplines herself to deliver world-class research and training programs; and Denise, who is highly energetic, productive, and influential, but a surprising number of her projects get sidelined, defunded, or abandoned. Remember, mine are likely to be different than yours—so be sure to choose the people and traits you admire. While it is fine to choose famous people or people you do not know, do include at least one person you know personally.

First, next to each name write three qualities that reflect the trait or skill you most notice about that person's ability. Here are my examples.

James

1. Fully acknowledges what is happening, feels it, and then chooses what to do.

2. Doesn't let the setback cause anger, but instead propel him to a solution.

3. Remains compassionate and cheerful, both optimistic in general and, specifically, hopeful.

Michelle

1. Ready for a challenge. She doesn't back away from a fight—but also doesn't cause conflict.

2. Is willing to be convinced if someone else has a better idea or is compelling.

3. Shares with others when she has good fortune.

Denise

1. Deals with what is on her plate right away.

2. Is flexible and forgiving in her way of responding.

3. Keeps an upbeat attitude.

Now let's look at how each person might respond to the four essential questions of a flexible mindset.

1. How might each person answer the first two questions: *What is happening?* and *What do I need to do?*

    James: He does a thorough analysis of what needs to be done first—including getting opinions.

    Michelle: Asks for feedback on her thinking up front.

    Denise: Gathers a good deal of information on her own—then asks for feedback.

2. How does each person deal with the second question: *What am I able to do?*

    James: Gets pro and con opinions on his chosen path(s). Also does this for others in a selfless way.

    Michelle: After she thinks things through and identifies her options, she checks in with others and will be forthcoming with her opinion when they ask.

    Denise: Listens to others' needs and rationale for action, as if she is gathering information for her current or future situation. Asks questions to clarify what other people are saying.

3. How does each follow through with monitoring the last question: *Is it working?*

    James: Very willing to experiment and test the chosen path, and change it if it isn't working.

Michelle: As her process shows signs of working, she expands it into other areas and shares it with others so they can use it. She does this very quickly once she knows it is working.

Denise: Stays hopeful and looks for the successes, while not ignoring the failures.

In your journal, make three comments about what you notice that is common to all three. This should highlight the features of a flexible mindset that you are ready to develop.

The list below highlights what I find essential in creating a flexible attitude for resilience. Make a list of what is important to *you* from the chosen people.

1. All invest heavily in researching options upon encountering a setback.

2. They keep their eyes on the prize, focus on having a positive attitude, and stay empowered.

3. They're willing to abandon a path if a better way presents itself— showing the capacity for ongoing monitoring.

Finally, make a chart like the one below and identify three things you've learned about what makes for a flexible mindset and resilience, and what you feel contributes to lack of resilience.

Resilient and Flexible Mindset	Lack of Resilience
Preparation and analysis are vital to creating many options. When there is a setback, they focus on what options will help them move forward.	Giving up easily when confronted with a challenge, and not thinking through alternatives. Being stuck with a defeatist attitude.
Focus on the future, with a positive attitude. Making things happen, not just letting things happen.	The pain and difficulty of the moment can overwhelm, preventing taking action.
Being willing to change thinking if the situation demands it.	Being too rigid with the choice made to deal with the issue. Not being open to change.

What did you find during your comparison? For me, preparation and readiness stood out. The role models paused, thought deeply about the next steps, and took responsibility for making things happen. Yet they were not so stubborn as to insist on sticking to their plan. When better alternatives were introduced, they readily adopted them. This highlighted that I need to keep my sense of despair and defeatism at bay, gather my resolve, and keep looking at the best options to continue.

What did your comparison yield? Whatever the answer, you now have your flexibility mindset workout routine. Just like grabbing the yoga mat, or stretching when you wake up, this becomes the preparation for keeping your mind limber and agile.

The key to cultivating flexibility is to have options available. I often use the image of a stream of water flowing over a rock. The water isn't impeded by the obstacle—it just goes around it.

I've been training and supervising therapists for more than 35 years, and when we talk about places in therapy where you can get stuck, I invite the therapists or students to think of three ways to move forward— not just one. This gives them flexibility and options at these difficult points.

This is my encouragement to you, when you get stuck in life. Pause for thought, determine what strengths you bring to the situation, and then generate a few options for moving forward, and choose one. More than just making you more resilient—cultivating flexibility gets you ready for the good life. As Joseph Campbell explains: "We must be willing to let go of the life we planned so as to have the life that is waiting for us."

In the next chapter, you'll learn a little bit more about what awaits. We'll turn our attention to how optimists can harvest positive emotions from a future self.

CHAPTER 5

OPTIMISM: Apply Perspective to Your Past and Future

My barn having burned down, I can now see the moon.

—Mizuta Masahide (17th-century
Japanese poet and samurai)

Think of a time you were excited about an upcoming event—something that you greatly anticipated, like a vacation, birthday celebration, trip to the theater, or visit from a friend. In touch with the positive emotions of expectation, you drifted easily into the future to sample what the experience would be like. You were in the here and now, but leaning into what you believed lay ahead filled you with anticipation. This shows that how you think about the future changes your experience of the present.

As Zen master Thich Nhat Hanh said, "The best way to take care of the future is to take care of the present moment." Your current state of mind can either cast a shadow in front of you—or light your way forward. In an optimistic state of mind, there is an alignment between the positive vision we have and how we feel. Feeling good about what is to come is the province of the optimist. It is the expectation that good things will happen.

Optimism is intriguing, because a positive forecast is linked with better outcomes. This has shown to be the case in many areas, such as physical health,[126] cardiac events,[127] work/life satisfaction,[128] and college performance.[129] Notably, the opposite is also true: Pessimism, or the tendency to feel negative about the future, predicts unfavorable outcomes. The evidence is just as strong as with optimism: negative thinking harms our well-being.[130] The reality of these findings for optimists and pessimists could be summed up in the words of the poet Allen Ginsberg: "You are what you think about all day."

Our inner HERO of hope, empowerment, resilience, and optimism is a treasure trove of positivity possibilities. In this chapter, as we investigate this final element of psychological capital—optimism—you will get a clearer picture of how each component of psychological capital uniquely contributes to the positivity effect, and where they overlap. This is because the positivity effect comes into play whenever we limit negativity while using various ways to generate positive emotions, to form better options.

When we consistently downregulate the negative and upregulate the positive, our perception will forecast a brighter future—increasing the likelihood of influencing our reality. We are optimistic when the perception informs expectations that are more positive than negative. We see a better future when the lens we see the world through isn't dark.

Let's look more closely at how hope and optimism are often confused or combined. You will recall that hope is the regulation of perception, in which we believe we can change the future. Hope and hopefulness highlight our sense of agency—the belief that we can make something happen. When we initiate this belief, a negative or uncertain belief about a situation or condition is transformed from hopeless to hopeful. Recall the discussion of how this means that the manure (negativity and uncertainty) in our life brings the nitrogen for growth (hope), and we thrive as a result. Hope is different from optimism because hope is specific to what we believe *we can do* to impact the future.

Optimism is a *general expectation* that things will work out. This is different from what you believe you can do to make things happen. This might sound like a slight difference, and its importance is hampered by everyday usage, as most of us use *hope* and *optimism* interchangeably. But they are not the same. As leading researcher on grit and perseverance Dr. Angela Duckworth has noted, "'I have a feeling tomorrow will be better' is different from 'I resolve to make tomorrow better.'"[131] The first is optimism, the second hope.

Consider a common thread that is evident in all aspects of HERO: *What you believe is what you achieve.* To cultivate each aspect, you have engaged specific interventions, like shifting your attention toward positivity, and, in doing so, transforming your beliefs. If you focus on the negative, you limit your choices from which to make decisions about the future. If you focus on the positive, the balance tips to noticing and feeling good about what is possible. The result is a regulation of perception that is guided by what you focus on.

The positivity effect reduces rumination about what is negative and uncertain while increasing what fills you up emotionally—increasing creative possibilities.[132] Difficulties become challenges, and crises create opportunities. You move toward each difficulty with a renewed and replenished sense of the available options. Each aspect of HERO that we have explored so far offers you specific ways to facilitate this transition.

- *Hope* arises when you believe you can make specific changes in the future.

- *Empowerment* develops a reserve of successfully made positive changes that you can draw on to enhance your confidence.

- *Resilience* draws on a flexible mindset to accurately assess a setback and offer a broader range of positive options to apply and experiment with.

- *Optimism* cultivates the expectation that good things are to come.

To understand how all of this works in practical terms, think about how your day unfolds. It presents you with endless choices, challenges, and problems to solve. You rely on habits to streamline your efforts and spontaneous problem-solving to cope with obstacles.

After the alarm wakes you up, you move into a sequence of well-rehearsed actions and morning habits that help launch your day. You drink coffee or tea, get in the shower, check the messages on your phone, and select your wardrobe. Yet each of these habits introduces a potential vulnerability into your scheme. You are out of coffee, the shower water doesn't get hot, your phone isn't charged, or you forgot to pick the clothes up from the cleaners.

Expectations and outcomes are guide rails that move you along your day. You start and stop, adjust, and do what you can to move on. You are a risk-assessment machine and, at any moment, can throw your hands in the air and give up. Yet you also can develop greater control, confidence, courage, and certainty—the four effects of hope, empowerment, resilience, and optimism.

As we unpack what optimism brings to the table in this chapter, you will notice that these features of psychological capital involve objectives that produce an effect. These four elements of psychological capital are not random, short-lived exercises to feel good. They are your way to access sustainable well-being. The aim of each is a resource, facilitated by action. The four verbs that go with each objective are: choose, capitalize, cultivate, and convert. To initiate psychological capital, effort is needed.

The Long-Term Effects of Optimism

Just as we've looked at specific interventions to increase hope, empowerment, and resilience, we'll now investigate positive interventions to increase an optimistic attitude. The interventions you'll learn can unlock optimism's power for you.

Optimism may be one of the most significant indicators of a longer life. It has been shown to keep people from getting depressed and to help them have more robust immune systems.[133] In one study, optimism predicted a lower mortality rate over four years.[134] In another, the same finding emerged after 40 years.[135] Optimism is ultrapractical, as it has broad implications for boosting resilience, physical and emotional well-being, and positive aging[136] (the process of developing and maintaining the functional ability that enables well-being in older age[137]). Optimism has an expansive influence on so many factors because being optimistic helps generate more coping strategies to overcome problems.

Think back to your adolescence and how it impacted your adult experiences. If you acted out of fear, this likely restricted your options. If you had the positivity associated with optimistic thinking, that may have broadened and built coping resources and led you to make more significant effort and commitment to reaching your goals. This is because our capacity for thinking positively or negatively develops early on.

Adults tend to get frustrated with "disengaged" teenagers who are not focused on doing much. It has been shown that when adolescents have negative expectations, their disengagement from trying to overcome difficulties is progressive and cumulative. It's also true that any of us will become disengaged whenever problems seem impossible.[138] Although there has been an increase in depression across all age-groups, adolescents are further ahead of this alarming trend,[139] which is also true for suicide.[140]

This book is for you, an adult, but imagine if you had been encouraged to develop healthy thinking habits as a young person. This is no different than learning about the advantages of eating well; awareness of emotional nourishment is just as important to understand as proper nutrition is.

The longer negative thinking takes root, the more work there is to undo it. This is why I encourage you to share what you learn with the 10- to 19-year-olds in your life. Recent research shows that positive expectations and the experience of more positive emotions in adolescents made them more resilient over a year later. Furthermore, those who were more resilient flourished more in subsequent years.

For any of us, adolescents included, to have a better future, we must learn to imagine one. As William James declared: "Believe that life is worth living, and your belief will help create the fact."

Imagining Your Way into Optimism

How do you think about who you will be in the future? Research shows that imagining a future self that has arrived at a desirable station in personal, relational, and professional aspects of life has many positive implications. It boosts positive affect and positive expectations.[141] Further, specific findings show that positive expectations decrease depression and anxiety, increase flow, reduce pain, reduce negativity, lessen health symptoms, increase self-esteem, increase positive emotions, improve physical and mental health, decrease hopelessness, increase happiness, and, importantly, increase optimism.[142] Also, evidence shows that no therapist or coach is needed. The effects of doing the following exercise are equally positive, however you do it.[143] Reading and following instructions, like the ones to come, will work as well on your own as in my office.

Many psychological interventions have been designed to boost optimism, but this one stands above others: Best Possible Self (BPS), which involves imagining your best possible life in the future. Such fantasy visualization might appear to be like frivolous role-playing, but a simple five-minute imagination exercise in thinking about oneself being happy and thriving in the future has been shown to sustainably boost positivity and optimism.[144]

When Laura King developed BPS in 2001,[145] it was already known that writing about upsetting and negative topics improved mental and physical well-being. At that time, there was a shift in thinking about the exploration of writing about *positive* experiences. King drew on the work of another writing researcher, James Pennebaker, and developed BPS. The intervention was used to upregulate positive emotions and compared to the disclosive technique of writing about one's trauma.[146]

Findings revealed that the BPS intervention produced the *same benefits* on health as writing about traumatic events—without people needing to relive and rehash the trauma to get relief. It was shown to be less upsetting than writing about traumatic events and significantly increased positive mood and well-being. These results have now been well established.[147]

Now you can gain the same (and in some cases better) results through an easier and more beneficial process. The BPS experiments demonstrate how you can use a positive, engaging, meaningful exercise that is just as powerful, without stirring up a bunch of negativity. In many ways, this shift to using positive interventions and activating positive emotions, rather than trying to manage only your negativity, is at the heart of the positivity effect. By focusing on increasing positive emotions, you will naturally reduce the negative.

You can do the following exercise at any time, in any state of mind. Research shows that it doesn't matter where your mood is at for a positive intervention such as the Best Possible Self to be effective. When they measured participants' mood before doing the BPS exercises, they determined that whether you started in a good mood or bad, with a pessimistic or optimistic attitude, it did not matter. The engagement in the BPS exercise improved initially and in an ongoing way.[148, 149]

The power of the Best Possible Self seems to be continually affirmed by a wide variety of research showing the intervention can be effective whether done by using imagination, writing, or talking. Additionally, repeating the BPS intervention makes it more effective.[150]

EXPLORATION: Savoring the Future—the Best Possible Self in Action

In this exercise, you will think about all the domains of your life and imagine that everything has worked out as well as it could have. You will imagine that your career, relationships, hobbies, academic work, health, financial standing, recognition, and satisfaction with your life are all working in ways that inspire a deep sense of appreciation and gratitude.

If you feel that your current life is far from the life you want, it may take some doing to nudge yourself to picture this best possible future. But suspend any judgment and emphasize the particulars of what you would like to have happen. The more specific and creative you are, the better. If your Best Possible Self is driving a high-quality car, imagine the vehicle's make, model, year, and color. If you are involved in a magnificent relationship, write down the name and character of the person you have the relationship with. Details tend to help.

To do this exercise, you'll need your journal to write in. Please try and do this exercise now, as it will help you understand precisely how the BPS works.

The best way to think about doing this exercise is by beginning with a nonjudgmental view of your current self and self-compassion and acceptance about where you are. As mentioned above, you will want to focus on a desirable future self in the domains of personal, relational, and professional ways.

There are four steps you are going to take to access the BPS.

1. Take a moment to decide how far you'll look into the future: 3 years? 5 years? 10 years? Think about who your Best Possible Self is then. Get clear about how this future would look through personal, relational, and professional lenses. Even more importantly, start to *feel* what it is like to be this way. Take a moment to create and savor this vision. Focus on what it would feel like, what people would be present, and what you would be doing.

2. Write this down in your journal, adding details as they come to mind. Research shows that the more you can describe and focus on these positive features, the better.[151] Consider devoting a page in your journal to personal aspects, another page to relational aspects, and a third page to professional aspects.

3. After writing, place an empty chair in front of the one you are sitting in. Imagine your future BPS sitting in that other chair. Notice how you feel. Then reverse roles by sitting in the BPS chair. From this chair, read the descriptions of your life from the journal—out loud. Begin with the sentence: "I am your Best Possible Self and I...."

4. You will need to record yourself so you can listen later, so for this step you may want to use the voice app on your cellphone. First, write down a list of questions you want to ask your BPS—anything you like, such as: *How does it feel to be where you are? How did you do so much? Do you have advice for me?*

    When you are ready, turn on your recording app and ask one question. Then reverse roles by switching seats, become the

BPS, and answer. You may be surprised by what your BPS has to say. To recall what the BPS said, the recorder comes in handy. Allow the question-and-answer dialogue to continue naturally, and take a few minutes to get to know your BPS.

After as many exchanges as you'd like, end the scene by sitting in the chair that signifies who you are now. Thank the BPS, and then write what this experience was like in your journal. If you have trouble recalling the answers, please listen to the voice recording. The purpose of having the encounter in this way is to give you access to the part of yourself that believes in you, and then to write it down, so you can remember and use the insights made available through the process.

At the core of savoring your best possible future is a principle first noted, as many things were, by William James: "There is a law in psychology that if you form a picture in your mind of what you would like to be, and you keep and hold that picture there long enough, you will soon become exactly as you have been thinking." This promise can be highly motivating.

Let's root out other ways that the negative thinking of pessimism can infiltrate your mind so that you can find the right optimistic balance.

Your Explanatory Style

Optimism and pessimism are opposite styles. Interestingly, scientists classify whether you are an optimist or pessimist based on how you explain what happens to you. How do you explain positive and negative events in your life? Both happen, but your explanatory style can determine a rosy or dismal outlook.

The explanatory styles for pessimists and optimists differ along three dimensions: the degree to which they explain a situation as permanent, pervasive, or personal. Here are descriptions of all three, as seen by a pessimist, followed by an optimist.

Perspective	Good Situation	Bad Situation
Pessimist	*Temporary* (they see the cause of that event as short-lived) *Isolated* (the cause of that situation is specific to that event only) *External* (the cause of that event is a consequence of other people or the situation itself)	*Permanent* (when something bad happens, the feeling will last forever) *Pervasive* (the event will affect all areas of their life) *Personal* (they alone are at fault)
Optimist	*Permanent* (when something good happens, the feeling will last forever) *Pervasive* (the event will affect all areas of their life) *Personal* (they alone are responsible)	*Temporary* (they see the cause of that event as short-lived) *Isolated* (the cause of that situation is specific to that event only) *External* (the cause of that event is a consequence of other people or the situation itself)

Optimists exaggerate the good and minimize the bad. Pessimists do precisely the opposite. Of course, people can be realists, accepting a situation as it is and dealing with it accordingly. But in any case, these perspectives represent different default perceptions and explanations, which reveals features of your character. The sense of "This is who I am" results from how you explain how and why things happen to you. If you believe this is who you are, it becomes your identity and how you see the world. Your explanation for why something happened to you in the past becomes how you believe life will unfold for you in the future. Your explanation becomes your expectation.

As the chart shows, optimism can be an extreme state when unbalanced. Negative thinking, pessimism, contingency planning, and fear all have their essential place and value. All of the problems associated with them have to do with overuse, not their inherent worth. We need them to survive. In some instances, it is important to worry—say, about topics like *Should I steal from my employer, have an affair, or cheat on my taxes?* (These are not multiple-choice options, by the way.)

We should indeed worry about the consequences of our actions. Even with all the research about its power, the positivity effect is not designed to replace negative thinking entirely, but rather to restore balance. We do not want to obliterate negative thinking, contingency thinking, fear, and pessimism; they all have tremendous value when used at the right time in the correct dosage. In some professions—such as being a lawyer—pessimism is highly valued.

Learning the Balance of Pessimism from Lawyers

As a group, lawyers are pessimistic. This can be a very good thing, because it is the very nature of their work—to worry about what could go wrong and help their clients prepare. This pessimistic and contingency planning style has been known for quite a while,[152] and while this label may not serve other professions well, it does lawyers.

Not all lawyers will have difficulties in their lives; some flourish and thrive. But those who have not yet managed their pessimistic perspective in other areas of their life may be at risk. This is because it is their job to worry, think about contingencies, and expect things to not go well. There is evidence that those with this style of thinking choose law school. The training and demands of their education make them ripe candidates for depression, difficulties with self-regulation, and a fixed mindset.[153] The incidence of problematic drinking and depression is often higher for lawyers than for the general population,[154] and abuse of drugs and alcohol often begins in law school.[155]

I have had the privilege to work as a trial lawyer consultant, a mental health adviser for law firms and institutions, and a speaker on well-being to some prestigious law schools. I have tremendous admiration for the work lawyers do, and for the unique psychological traits I have observed firsthand.[156] This draws them to their chosen profession.

We have learned something about the power of expectations on well-being from studying lawyers, which can offer you helpful context. It has been found that when pessimistic lawyers have a specific expectation that something will happen, and then it doesn't, this dashed expectation does the most damage.[157] If the highly expected, promised, all-but-assured future isn't realized, the pain is greatest. Feelings of betrayal are strong. For example, research has shown that when lawyers expect to become partners, those wrongly assuming partnership to be a foregone conclusion suffer most. On the other hand, those pessimistic lawyers who aspire to a partnership that never materializes come through essentially unscathed.

According to the researchers, when lawyers have aspiration without expectation and their hope goes unrealized, there's no discernible impact on depressive symptoms. But "among the many possible selves lawyers envisage, falling short of the 'probable' future self is more distressing than failing to become the 'like-to-be' future self."[158]

This means that a missed *probability* will hurt much more than a missed *possibility*. When an expectation is in hand and lost, it will have a different impact than when a desired outcome isn't fulfilled.

You Can Age Better and More Happily with Optimism

The 2009 Nobel Prize–winning research in Physiology or Medicine was awarded jointly to Elizabeth H. Blackburn, Carol W. Greider, and Jack W. Szostak, "for the discovery of how chromosomes are protected by telomeres and the enzyme telomerase."[159] These exceptional researchers revealed how every cell in your body is listening to your thoughts, and how this can have a lasting effect, one way or another, throughout a life span.[160] Let's look at this closely, to explore how optimism works physically.

Although aging is unavoidable, how well we age is within our control. People who have lived a long, healthy, and successful life can teach us about the positivity effect and what it takes to thrive mentally and physically. Studies show that hope,[161] empowerment (self-efficacy),[162] resilience,[163] and optimism[164] are factors leading to longevity and satisfaction with life. It isn't just our genes that determine our capacity to thrive and flourish—it's the degree to which we manage stress and anxiety.

Each threat appraisal you make triggers a fight-or-flight response, as your whole system gets ready to deal with the perceived threat. This causes stress and anxiety, as your body goes on high alert to deal with the threat. In particular, chronic, cumulative stress is associated with higher levels of the stress hormone adrenocorticotropic hormone (ACTH), more cortisol in the blood, and elevated blood sugar levels. The elevated blood sugar levels contribute to insulin resistance (which is why we turn to food as a stress-coping mechanism), and not dealing adequately with stress increases inflammation. Over time, our capacity for coping breaks down, and so does our body. This deterioration is what causes disease and aging.[165]

The widespread deterioration happens from stress because the cells in the body deteriorate.[166] *Telomeres* are like the aglets on our shoelaces; they are what hold together the tips of our chromosomes to protect them from decompensating, breaking down, and deteriorating.[167, 168] Telomeres also help to regulate how our cells replicate themselves. In brief, telomere length will determine the health of our cells, which in turn determines our physical well-being. Telomeres have such an effect because they are part of every cell in our body. Essentially, if we are aging well, the telomere "aglets" have protected our cells.

Telomeres are made from a complex protein known as *shelterin* and have been found to shorten through deterioration as we age. Each time a cell replicates, this deterioration occurs, caused by a deficiency in an enzyme known as *telomerase*[169]—which is responsible for making the telomeres. Our cells will continue to replicate until they can no longer do so. *Cell senescence* (death of a cell) happens through telomere erosion; it is irreversible and leads to diseases like cancer, dementia, diabetes, and more.[170] We have more diseases as we age because our cells are less robust and can no longer replicate themselves.

If you want to slow down the aging process and limit the diseases you get and how long you have them, the number-one thing to do is prevent telomeres from shortening.[171] Telomeres are most affected by three factors:

chronic inflammation, oxidative stress, and psychological stress.[172, 173] For this book, I'll focus on how stress affects the length of telomeres.

In the 2017 book *The Telomere Effect: A Revolutionary Approach to Living Younger, Healthier, Longer,* Elizabeth Blackburn and Elissa Epel[174] offer a great many ideas of what can contribute to telomere maintenance. In particular, they identify the harmful effects of stress and rumination on telomere length, and share healthy suggestions for cultivating resilient thought patterns and other essential ways to increase well-being. They make a clear point that our cells are listening to our thoughts.

As it turns out, managing your thoughts may be the most direct way to influence your telomeres' length. One study[175] compared DNA methylation, another aspect of telomere maintenance, between long-term mindfulness meditators and a control group of non-meditators. The 17 long-term male and female meditators had to have at least 10 years of daily 60-minute meditation sessions under their belt to be included in the study. They were matched and compared to controls who had no meditation experience. In this cross-sectional study (measuring participants at their different ages at the time of the research), it was demonstrated that the controls showed the expected inverse relationship between their age and telomere length—meaning that the older they were, the shorter their telomere length. However, the researchers made a powerful discovery: *"Notably, age showed no association with telomere length in the group of long-term meditators."* Meditation lessened the effects of aging. The meditators also scored high on life satisfaction, happiness, and resilience; they scored lower on avoidance, anxiety, and depression measures. This shows how the meditators' practices—which involved directly managing their thought process, mindfully suspending self-judgment, and increasing curiosity about their mind—directly improved their well-being and slowed their cellular aging. The long-term meditators in this study reveal how you can affect your overall well-being by managing your thoughts.

And you don't have to meditate for an hour a day for ten years to get results. You have choice and control over your thoughts. Every time you can catch yourself thinking negatively, ask if these thoughts are best for your mental health and well-being. Remember, your cells are listening, so the answer you give might influence how well and how long you live.

Other researchers have shown that any effort at emotion regulation and self-control will positively impact stress and aging. In much the same way as was found with the meditators, stronger emotional regulation efforts (such as the explorations you are doing to increase the positivity effect) were found to prevent the effect of stress on aging. It is key to understand that stress itself decreases our cognitive and emotional regulation abilities.[176, 177] You need to steer your thoughts away from ruminating negatively as soon as possible, before it hijacks your brain and body, making it even more difficult to regulate your thoughts and emotions.

Cultivating an Enduringly Optimistic Mindset

An Austrian neurologist, psychiatrist, and Holocaust survivor, Viktor Frankl was the author of *Man's Search for Meaning* and the originator of logotherapy, a form of existential analysis. In the postscript to his book in 1984, he added "The Case for a Tragic Optimism."

As a Holocaust survivor, Frankl was forced to deal with some of the most tragic aspects of a life of pain, guilt, and death—yet he maintained a sense of meaning despite these tragic aspects. Under these extreme conditions of chronic stress, Frankl believed in human potential. Optimism in the face of tragedy "presupposes the human capacity to creatively turn life's negative aspects into something positive or constructive. In other words, what matters is to make the best of any given situation."[178]

As we have already learned, more creative possibilities and solutions spring from having more positive emotions available. Frankl's work centered around transforming feelings, such as turning suffering into a human achievement and accomplishment.

EXPLORATION: Finding Your Tragic Optimism

In this exercise, please use your journal. We'll begin with an exploration of three of Frankl's fundamentals.

1. For this first exploration, please write down the single most challenging event you have had to cope with in your life. Think of this

as a pivot point. Here are the elements to review as you write out your answer.

- Was there an expectation that didn't happen? If so, what was the expectation, and what was the reason it didn't occur?

- Was this event something you felt responsible for, or did it happen because of others?

- How did your life change because of it? What made your life more complex, what happened that was a surprise, and what may have even contributed to you accomplishing or achieving something?

- Can you view the event as part of a larger life story? What good things have come into your life due to the experience?

2. After identifying and responding to the first prompt, think of what it took, following the tragedy, to change yourself for the better.

- What courage was needed to help you not just cope, but move toward healing?

- Did you have to overcome any feelings of guilt as you made this change? How did you do this?

- Were there surprises in the growth experienced? Were you able to see this significant event differently over time? If so, what was the transition in your perception that took place?

- How has your life improved since this event?

3. Finally, write about what new actions resulted from this event.

- Did the event cause you to take a new path of action?

- Did it provide an incentive?

- Were you able to turn the experience into something good?

- Did any of your relationships improve?

- Were friends and family valued more?

- Did you spend more time helping others?

As you step back from this exercise and review your notes, write a summary statement of how this exercise has changed your perspective on the event.

If you now had to describe to a stranger what an optimistic mindset is, what would you say? As you respond, draw on your personal experience and solutions from the questions in this exercise to provide a description.

The Case for Balancing by Emphasizing Optimism

Negative thinking, fear, and pessimism are not the culprits, per se—but their chronic presence and volume are. Unfortunately, out-of-proportion negativity has hijacked not only our brains, but also the profession of psychology up until recent history. The dominance of the medical model in psychology has left the science and practice of psychology with a dismal track record. Seeing people's difficulties as symptoms that need to be removed was, at best, a myopic perspective on what it means to be emotionally healthy. Somehow focusing only on reducing or eliminating the negativity was seen as the goal, with restoring the status quo as "healing."

This perspective has overlooked the obvious. First, the medical approach simply doesn't work—the very model that psychology and psychotherapeutic intervention were based on is a failure at improving well-being. This is because well-being was defined as only the absence of symptoms, and the medicines do not work to do that.[179] The use of medicine to prevent relapse continues to be systematically poor, with relapse rates continuing to increase after treatment.[180] With this approach, we never get a chance to improve well-being, because the goal of reducing symptoms alone hasn't worked. Psychotherapy approaches also have incredibly high relapse rates, even for the best and most effective CBT therapies.[181]

The positivity effect is at the center of this renaissance in treatment. Recent meta-analysis studies highlight the failure of the standard approaches and advocate that the optimal treatment protocol for depression is adding well-being therapy (WBT).[182] Adding WBT following CBT and all of CBT's modifications, such as *mindfulness-based cognitive therapy*, makes the intervention more effective and longer lasting.

WBT is a short-term psychotherapeutic technique[183] based on the six dimensions of psychological well-being:[184] self-acceptance, autonomy, environmental mastery, personal growth, purpose in life, and positive relationships. These are all components of the positivity effect.

Throughout this book, you have been learning elements that align with these well-being features and a host of other positive interventions known to support, activate, and promote positivity. WBT, unlike the traditional approaches, targets something known as *euthymia*, which is a normal, tranquil mental state or mood.[185] It has patients keep a diary of moments of well-being.

Research shows that suppression (blocking or limiting negativity for regulation), when balanced with a move toward a positive mood and serenity, has therapeutic value.[186] Additionally, WBT has successfully decreased vulnerability to relapse while improving recovery levels for those with a psychiatric disorder. When you add positivity to the mix, you get a dynamic result that tips the scale in favor of sustainable well-being.

As we complete our journey on optimism, we will look toward maintaining and sustaining the positivity effect. In the next chapter, we'll look at post-traumatic growth and two ways you can live with great passion.

CHAPTER 6

Tools for Sustaining the Positivity Effect

Your task is not to foresee the future, but to enable it.

—Antoine de Saint-Exupéry

Your emotional reactions can sometimes surprise you—even as they are entirely effective. Perhaps you were assertive with a stranger when they tried to cut in front of you in line. Spoke up at a meeting with a contradictory point of view. Laughed when most people thought you would be angry. Responded to a difficult person with a detachment that allowed you to cope with the encounter effectively.

In moments like these, we may marvel at ourselves for finding the courage and spontaneity to deviate from our expected emotional response. There's a swell of self-reliance when we do something unexpected in a tough situation. At that moment, it can change how we feel about ourselves and how we relate to others, for the better.

When these things happen, they are part of a larger skill set known as *emotional self-regulation*. Rather than responding with a knee-jerk reaction, you have a more evolved or thoughtful response. You allow other more creative, better options to come through; you choose the right emotion for the situation. With emotional self-regulation, your emotions go from one-size-fits-all to custom-tailored.

Naturally hopeful, empowered, resilient, and optimistic people are capable of emotional regulation and have a dynamic, teachable pattern. They know how to cultivate their psychological capital and facilitate their inner HERO. Pushing out of a bad mental and emotional place is half the work, as they get away from what is excessively negative and depleting. The other half is *staying out*, by using positivity, in a way that compels and pulls them forward. At the heart of this push and pull is their ability to self-regulate.

Pushing away, suppressing, and reducing symptoms has been the primary focus of psychological and medical interventions throughout the history of science. Specifically, we have only attempted to reduce and downregulate negativity, ameliorate suffering, and stop symptoms. But this effort at emotional regulation is only half of what's needed. It's like trying to drive a car by only using the brake. This approach is outmoded, ineffective, and not in keeping with the best that science has to offer.

To contain the rising tide of fear and despondency, depression, anxiety, and hopelessness, we need to add tools that facilitate and upregulate positivity. In order to not get stuck at the bottom of a hill, you need to manage both the brake and gas pedals. You cannot use the same ill-fated approach if you want things to change.

Treating Symptoms That Keep Getting Worse

The failure of this approach is obvious when you look at the rising mental health issues in schools, at work, and at home. There is an excessive epidemic of depression and anxiety among all age-groups in all settings around the globe, with sadness, stress, and worry reaching all-time worldwide highs. According to Gallup's 2022 Global Emotions Report, the trend for this situation is getting worse.[187] The Gallup report highlights three important, alarming tendencies:

1. People are having more negative experiences and fewer positive ones.

2. Stress, sadness, and worry are at their highest recorded levels.

3. People do not feel rested and experience less joy than at any other time in history.

This prevalence, however, doesn't mean you can't do something about it. These tendencies are likely to have happened because treatments have been like only using the brakes—downregulating negative emotions. Now we need to power up, from the bottom of the hill.

Only downregulating negativity has offered no way to accelerate positive emotions, and no reliable way to *prevent* depression, anxiety, and other mental health issues from recurring. It offers too little to help you cope with difficult feelings as they arise. Downregulating also excludes becoming proactive about your future well-being. When a strategy does not help you prevent relapse, cope, or be proactive, it is time to change it. This is something the global community needs to do—and something you can start doing for yourself now.

By way of analogy, let's look at how a scientific solution for an increasingly difficult problem did not help—but actually made the situation worse. For about forty years, between 1870 and 1910, science offered a solution for dealing with fire—a nifty contraption called a fire extinguisher. Rather than a bucket brigade, it suppressed the blaze by using glass "fire grenades" to put out the flames. Held by wall brackets, these decorative glass-blown bulbs were often filled with salt water or carbon tetrachloride. When a fire started, the bulbs were thrown at the base of the fire, where they would shatter and release the contents to extinguish the flames. The small amount of saltwater rarely did much, and the carbon tetrachloride was unhealthy if inhaled, ingested, or absorbed, because it was later found to be carcinogenic. Worse yet, when carbon tetrachloride hit the flames, the chemical heated up and became phosphene gas,[188] a toxic poison eventually used for chemical warfare.

These early fire extinguishers offered false security. They looked like a good idea but were inadequate, dangerous, and did nothing to help the real problem. When carbon tetrachloride was thrown at a flame, it took a problematic situation and made it worse. In a not-dissimilar way, antidepressants, designed to put out the fire of depression, haven't been as effective as promised, and are proven to increase the risk of suicide attempts and suicide.[189]

When the fire grenades suppressed the fire, it seemed more a random act of luck than a calculated intervention. Similarly, when marginally better CBT approaches have been successful, no one is certain why they work.[190] In spite of all the treatments available, there is no less depression and anxiety—but instead, more people are suffering than at any other time in history. Researchers and clinicians call this the *treatment-prevalence paradox.*[191] We have an embarrassing array of treatments for conditions that keep getting worse.

The old science of psychology and psychiatry attempted to put out emotional fires by throwing our version of glass grenades. The new science must provide faster-acting, more effective emotional fire extinguishers, while installing comprehensive sprinkler systems and well-designed, fire-proof buildings. The goals for mental health and well-being need to change as well. The mental health profession has been waiting for a fire to break out, then tossing glass bombs at it.

When you focus on cultivating power to prevent and cope with negativity while proactively increasing positivity and well-being, you learn how to put out the flames *and* build a flame-resistant, strong, happy psyche. You have the ability and tools to balance the full spectrum of your emotions. This is where we can learn from people with high psychological capital, who have harnessed the positivity effect. To put out fires, they have learned to regulate their perceptions and, as a result, manage their feelings through emotional self-regulation. To flourish in the face of a potential disaster, they've discovered how to rise from the ashes, which is post-traumatic growth (PTG). Let's look closely at both of these skills.

Effects of Emotional Self-Regulation

For you to understand emotional self-regulation and make changes in your well-being, you need to know how your emotions work, how you perceive them, and how you can transform them so that they help rather than hinder. But emotional literacy isn't taught in schools, at work, or at home, and the controversy about whether it should be is hotly debated.[192] Not understanding how your emotions function is at the very root of mental health problems. When you don't know how to self-regulate emotions, the negative ones will hijack your brain.

In schools, this causes conduct disorders, absenteeism, lack of motivation, poor grades, bullying, isolation, drug abuse, depression, aggression, and feelings of alienation. When emotional self-regulation and mental health needs are included as part of what schools offer, there is a tremendous impact—lowering health risk behaviors, psychiatric disorders, substance dependence, crime, and, eventually, unemployment.[193] In particular, teaching emotional self-regulation helps reduce suicide risk, use of cigarettes and marijuana, and abuse of prescription drugs.[194] Teaching only academic topics in school is a mistake that is being corrected,[195] but nowhere near as fast as it needs to happen.

As for work, focusing only on productivity is not enough. Tending to employees' well-being in a substantial, measurable, and impactful way is being called for from every sector because it is now necessary. At work, businesses that do not facilitate these skills in their employees experience higher rates of absenteeism, presenteeism, lack of productivity, and burnout.[196]

Although this book is for adults, these tools are also useful for children and adolescents. This work offers insight into how adults with high psychological capital got that way. Studies about what predicts student flourishing show that, along with decreased levels of anxiety and depression, it is the *combination* of HERO concepts *rather than individual* HERO constructs that makes the difference. While each has a unique contribution to well-being—using hope, empowerment, resilience, and optimism *together* has an additive effect.[197] Emotional and social self-regulation plays a key role in how the components of HERO are used in concert to orchestrate a better life early on, and the effect of this work continues into adulthood.[198] Using psychological capital interventions together is better than using each alone. You too can boost your psychological capital by using these new tools and interventions.

WOOP

A powerful technique pulls together the HERO elements through four steps: wish, outcome, obstacle, plan (WOOP). You generate a specific wish or goal, visualize the best outcomes, identify the obstacles to the goal, and generate "if…then" plans for overcoming the obstacles.[199] The unique contribution of this intervention is that it focuses on ways to deal with the obstacles to the goal—not just the goal. This technique has been used effectively as a way to self-regulate and facilitate self-discipline.[200]

Let's look at how the WOOP technique combines psychological capital.

1. The wish or goal, and the belief that you can achieve it, activates the feature of *hope*.

2. By thinking about the best outcomes, you engage your sense of *optimism* (similar to the Best Possible Self exercise in the previous chapter).

3. By identifying and anticipating the obstacles in your path, you cultivate *resilience*. Recall the quote at the beginning of chapter 4 by Marcus Aurelius: "The impediment to action advances action. What stands in the way becomes the way." This identifies the action to take to overcome the impediment.

4. Finally, making deliberate plans *empowers* you. It adds to your confidence that you can achieve the goal.

EXPLORATION: Self-Regulation through the WOOP Technique

In your journal, write down a goal you want to achieve. As always, please do this exercise now rather than skip it. To begin, choose a difficult but not catastrophic issue. For the purpose of the exercise, try to pick a goal that is relatively short-term, for which your motivation for achieving it is substantial. You would really like to see it happen, and it is more than a passing desire.

As an example, suppose you wanted to take three spin classes a week at the local gym. Here is what the WOOP outline might look like.

1. Wish: I want to take three 45-minute spin cycling classes each week at my gym.

2. Outcome: I will have more energy, feel better, and manage my weight. When I imagine how this will be in the future, I see myself feeling energetic, healthy, and fit.

3. Obstacle: My work schedule changes a lot and I might not be able to make it to all three classes.

4. Plan: When I can't make the cycling classes in person, I can still go to the gym and use the app to take a prerecorded class. Although I won't be in my favorite class, I'll still get the exercise I want.

What's your WOOP? Make a list of the four steps and fill them in for a wish you have. Then put the plan into operation for a week. See what results you get, and write down your thoughts on how this approach worked. Many people report that focusing on the obstacle part of the plan enhances their psychological capital. Somehow, identifying the problem and what can be done about it nurtures and inspires our psychological resources. What was your experience when working on your wish?

When we have physical pain, we may automatically become curious about its cause and remedies, and take measures to prevent it from happening again. But when there is emotional pain, it often almost immediately depletes the energy needed to explore ways to correct it. With physical pain, we may feel motivated to learn more about it and change it. With emotional pain, there is typically ignorance about what is causing it, combined with helplessness to make change happen. This is what my colleagues and I are trying to change.

The positivity effect highlights the ways in which focusing on HERO (hope, empowerment, resilience, and optimism) interventions shift your attention, alter your beliefs, and create an ability to regulate your perception. My hope is that the things we've covered so far are having an additive effect, as each of the interventions and transformations are added to your toolbox. Sudden extreme changes can run the risk of you burning out and getting pulled back into the vortex of negativity. You need tools you are familiar with to help you get out, stay out, and continually nourish your new crop of positive emotions. People with high levels of psychological capital know what it takes to flourish and thrive, even when the stakes are high.

Post-traumatic Growth Inspires Your Future

When two hijacked planes deliberately crashed into the Twin Towers of the World Trade Center on September 11, 2001, people unprepared for catastrophe had to react. The terrorist attack and its aftermath have been, and continue to be, deeply researched, as it provides a rare glimpse into survival instincts. Study of this and other traumatic events provides insight into a profoundly unique quality that was heretofore unexplored— *post-traumatic growth,* or PTG.

In their seminal 2004 article, Richard Tedeschi and Lawrence Calhoun laid out the concept of and research related to the phenomenon of post-traumatic growth. PTG is the experience of a positive change after a life crisis, which increases appreciation for life and prioritizing of personal relationships. It also can change priorities, improve personal-psychological strength, and deepen spiritual life.[201]

This response is of deep interest in the psychology community because it shows how and why traumatic events can become a *catalyst* for a profound expansion of personal development. Trauma is no longer considered the cause-and-effect trigger for PTSD. *Potentially traumatic events* show us that trauma may or may not follow.

With PTG, the potentially traumatic event can initiate transformation and growth. Theories and research about PTG transformation range from a complete change of personality,[202] to a change in the way individuals with PTG recall and then highlight their adaptive changes. By shifting perceptions to a narrative of personal growth, individuals who've experienced a trauma become capable of post-traumatic growth.[203]

What makes PTG important is that it is not simply a return to a former baseline. People don't go back to where they were before the trauma—they experience radical improvement. And they do it alongside their attempt to adapt to difficult circumstances that cause high levels of distress. What's more, post-traumatic *growth* is far more common than the trauma resulting in a psychiatric condition. Under the direst of circumstances, what doesn't kill us makes us grow.

Growth and suffering are part of adapting to negatively charged circumstances. With PTG, personal distress and growth coexist. The loss and incomprehensibility of the traumatic event often still remain, but the emphasis is on an orientation *toward the future*. The shift in perception goes beyond what was lost to include what the potential traumatic event means in terms of revised goals, cognitive schemes to attain them, and the motivation to do so. The result can be transformation and a deep change in how we function.

Emotional Self-Regulation Applied to Devastation

Growth is not the automatic result of trauma. A traumatic event doesn't *cause* one to grow psychologically. Rather, growth may be a reaction to the new reality emerging from psychological distress, which determines if PTG occurs or not. Not merely an intellectual or cognitive restructuring, this transformation is facilitated by a deeply emotional component. The powerful feelings and acknowledgment of the painful circumstances are used in the service of planning for the future. It isn't just thinking about the trauma differently that makes the change—it is being able to regulate emotional reactions that help shape a more growth-oriented future.

When potters begin to shape a ball of clay on a potter's wheel, they first press down on the clay to ensure it is anchored as it spins. This is like the intellectual and cognitive approach of coping with a traumatic event. We take what was handed to us and get it ready to be shaped into something useful. The very next thing the potter does is wet the clay and their hands. This is like adding emotional regulation. It is necessary to facilitate the process.

When trauma survivors rebuild their psyches, they live in two worlds: one of pain, loss, and devastation, and the other of what needs to be done to build a new life. With communities that rebuild after floods, earthquakes, and tornadoes, engineers study the structures that survived the event and plan rebuilding accordingly. Those wounded by trauma are themselves the survivors, and their own engineers.

I live at the Jersey Shore and moved into my house only months before Superstorm Sandy hit. The previous owners were interior decorators and engineers who had rebuilt the home to withstand the 100-year flood (the likelihood of an excessive flood, as set by the National Flood Insurance Program[204]) while keeping it aesthetically pleasing. They layered gardens with retaining walls from the dock on the water's edge and installed a 12-foot-capacity floating dock. They had pitched the home's backyard to create a higher-level setting for the home, and had made plans to install a water-powered backup sump pump. These unique inventions were powered by municipal water pressure and required no electricity or battery to run. The engineer highly recommended I complete their renovation by adding the pump, which I had never heard of before, to ensure the basement wouldn't flood. I did, only because of his insistence, and the job was completed the month before the storm.

When Sandy hit, the flume on the lake that separates the ocean from our body of water failed, and the lake filled quickly. I was evacuated for seven days. The level of devastation from the water damage to the area was beyond anything I'd ever seen, and anything that the area's population had ever had to cope with. In some cases, entire shore towns simply washed away.

Fearing the worst, when I returned I was surprised to find that the home was still intact and the basement dry—with the water-powered pump still running. Environmental Protection Agency (EPA) engineers, in the aftermath, determined that only the homes with this style of backup pumps, retaining walls, floating docks, and built on pilings survived. The building codes up and down the Jersey Shore changed as a result of the flood, to incorporate these insights.

In much the same way, trauma survivors can respond to devastation by rebuilding their psyches, to fortify themselves for the future in ways that make them less vulnerable and more prepared.

Post-traumatic growth is a genuinely long-term effect that happens to many people following a traumatic event. Yet this does not mean that they don't experience any negative reactions. Rather, *in spite of* being exposed to an emotionally shattering experience, they nevertheless experience psychological growth. Informed by the past, they rebuild the future.

How This Book Sets You Up for Post-traumatic Growth

What changes take place for those experiencing PTG? At the very top of the list is a greater appreciation for life. There is more gratitude, more often, for large and small things. But we don't have to wait for a traumatic event to reap the benefits of this practice. This is one reason why we began chapter 1 with a gratitude exercise. You can shift your perception of what is important, right now. As we learned in chapter 2 on hope, recalibrating goals brings you closer to experiencing the joy of achieving them.

PTG research shows that these survivors also develop warmer, more intimate relationships and have a greater sense of personal strength. As we explored in chapter 3 on empowerment, confidence comes from our decisions about what to look for in our brain's search engine. Individuals with PTG are searching for instances of growth to craft their narrative.

When new possibilities for one's life become evident, an individual with PTG uses the mechanics of resilience and optimism. This is why in chapter 4 on resilience, we explored the flexibility mindset, and in chapter 5 on optimism, you had a conversation with your Best Possible Self. Those devastated by life circumstances who use the pain to grow, have broken through to a better way to live. Although motivated by tremendous pain, they have left us blueprints to follow, so we can apply their skills to improve our lives. You don't need trauma to reap the benefits of struggling toward growth and well-being. You can learn from those whose courage has illuminated the path.

When you did the resilience exploration in chapter 4, you focused on *What is happening?* as a way to accurately appraise the situation. This helped you decide what option to pursue. As you explore PTG, you'll do something similar, by making an accurate assessment of what you're feeling. As you'll see, making a cognitive assessment of what is happening is different from making an emotional assessment.

EXPLORATION: Holding Difficult Feelings

In this exercise, we take a cue from the previous chapter's work on tragic optimism. You previously explored Viktor Frankl's thinking around how we can transform feelings, to turn suffering into a human achievement and accomplishment. I believe Frankl's work on tragic optimism created a platform for the research on PTG to shine through. The premise was there, and research continues to support it.

This exploration has three steps. Please read through all the steps to be certain that this exercise feels safe for you to do. If a difficulty happened very recently, there may be hidden obstacles. Do not push yourself. If at any point you feel it is too difficult for you to handle, please know you are the world's expert on you—and don't make yourself do anything that feels uncomfortable. The idea here is to recall a challenging scene and find a way to experience the feelings that allows you to not get overwhelmed by them. If, for any reason, this doesn't seem possible, please instead write down the reasons for this in your journal. This will go a long way toward your growth in coping with difficult emotions.

First, find a scene from your life where a difficult feeling began. Where did a feeling of betrayal, pain, trauma, dismay, or bewilderment emerge? Set the scene as though you were going to describe it in a play, screenplay, short story, or essay. As you craft the features of this scene, write them down in a paragraph. This is step 1.

1. Here is an example: *It was a warm summer day, and I was walking with my partner down a street in my neighborhood, on my way to*

a friend's house. We passed a neighbor and their familiar dog on a leash. I said hello, and as we walked past, the golden retriever made a sudden lunge at me, and I put my arm up to block him. He bit through my long-sleeve shirt, tearing painfully into the skin on my forearm. The pain was excruciating. The shock was overwhelming, and I was hurt and angry—a string of curse words streamed from my mouth. They immediately locked the dog in a nearby car. I could see the blood oozing through my shirt; the agony was nearly unbearable. When I saw the blood and felt my anger, I knew this was something I had to deal with—but I didn't have a plan. Something had happened that I couldn't avoid, ignore, or pretend didn't bother me.

Following this, review the intensity of the recalled emotion(s). This is step 2. It is common to have a swirl of feelings, and not necessarily one discrete emotion. Here is an example, following the above scene.

2. *The intensity of the physical pain seemed to fuel my anger, yet I was aware that I was watching my reaction, almost like it was happening to someone else. I felt anger, shock, and deep, throbbing pain where the bite was.*

Finally, in step 3, as you recall your feelings from the scene, hold what was felt, bring it into the current moment, and make space for it to be felt without judgment. The observer part of you that was recalling the event as it happened is now replaying the emotional tape. Bring yourself back to that moment, feel the feeling—and importantly, hold this feeling for inspection with no judgment.

At this moment, you want two things to happen. You need to both feel the feeling and provide the container for it to be held. You are both the observer and the feeling. What is it that you were feeling at the core of that moment? The answer is coming from the observer.

3. *As I recall the feelings of anger and shock, I was aware it felt like a type of betrayal. I don't think the word "betrayal" came into my mind—but the feeling did, and I remember scrambling to*

*understand it as I was thinking about the next thing I had to do to
take care of myself.*

To review, the three steps are 1) remembering the scene, 2) identifying and feeling the feelings, and then 3) recalling them into the present moment and observing and feeling them without judgment. This third one is a crucial element for transformation, as you are not trying to change the scene, launch countermeasures of thinking, or suppress it. You are letting it bubble up in your mind and then using your awareness to hold on to the memories from the scene for a brief time. Once you've done this—typically for 10 to 30 seconds—write down your experience in your journal.

If you can, allow yourself to do this exercise with the same memory a few times over several days.

Negative emotions transform when they are known and experienced in a way in which they do not hijack our minds and begin intrusive rumination. As you are able to evoke them and provide the awareness container for them to remain active, yet not harmful, you can learn how they function. Imagine a lobster trap a marine biologist might use to study the animal. You want the lobster to remain alive so you can study it, but you don't want it to harm you. Similarly, you can look at your painful emotions and not be harmed by them. In fact, your painful emotions can lead to beautiful results.

Pearls of Vulnerability

A delicate balance can occur when we hold negative emotions: we use vulnerability as a sense of strength. We are hurt and upset—and at the same time we struggle to find ways to cope. There is incongruity when a sudden, unexpected negative event triggers a response to endure and carry on. We may experience this as a meeting of opposites: pain and growth, limits and expansion, self-reliance and needing support, and helpful people mixed in with the inconsiderate, cruel, and inhumane.[205]

The recognition of these paradoxes is collectively known as *post-traumatic depreciation*. Along with the good comes the bad, and vice versa.

To cope with these polarities, trauma survivors with PTG use *dialectical thinking*.[206] Dialectical thinking is when two polar-opposite things (like vulnerability and strength) are held together in your awareness. This is a central feature in the findings about PTG and the literature on the relationship between wisdom and subjective well-being.[207] While the events that led to a difficult reaction are not desirable, there is goodness and growth that can come from having to face them.[208] By learning to hold difficult feelings, like you did for the previous exploration, you begin cultivating this process. Activate a memory that makes you vulnerable, then cultivate strength by rehearsing it while not being overwhelmed by it.

Our initial responses to a difficult circumstance tend to automatically be negative: intrusive ruminations, images, and thoughts. This immediate response of the mind to an outside, disruptive event is mirrored in oysters. When these mollusks have to cope with unwanted bits of sand or grit that float into their shell, they do so by coating the irritant with *nacre*, which makes up the oyster's inner shell. We know this inner shell as "mother of pearl," because the layers upon layers of nacre create pearls. This is a metaphor for how discomfort and irritation from an intrusive event can grow into a jewel.

Let's look at this even closer, because oysters also mirror the PTG process that leads to *permanent* transformation. There is a "before trauma" and "after trauma" state for the oyster, as there is for those with PTG. Pearls typically lodge permanently between the mantle (a membrane surrounding inner organs inside the two halves of the oyster shell) and the shell. This means that after an irritant gets in there, the inner world of the oyster is changed forever. The unwanted object causes growth.

This is also a psychological truth for individuals with PTG. Their dialectical process—of holding two opposite truths in mind—uses the irritation to create growth. Those with PTG work hard to close the gap between circumstances and optimal functioning. With survivors of trauma, being forced to disengage from previous goals and assumptions gives way to a new reality. Their inner world changes—and permanent growth comes from an unwanted event.[209]

Curiously, to continue the analogy, it is commonly assumed that oysters are unique in their ability to make pearls. What is less well-known is that most bivalves can make pearls, including surf clams, mussels, soft-shell clams, oysters, and scallops. Just as pearls are more typical than we may have thought, we are learning that PTG may be more common than initially imagined.

And the good that can come from difficulties isn't short-lived. Studies interviewing 9/11 survivors found that the vast majority of those who had direct experience in or near the World Trade Center—more than two-thirds—had tremendous psychological growth within an 18-month period following the event.[210] This means that even early on, there can be measurable PTG. But does it last? In the 2021 follow-up study, it was reported that fifteen years after 9/11, those with the same high level of exposure had had traumatic stress responses *and* PTG. We continue to create pearls long after the irritant has entered our shell.

Forces that fuel sustainable PTG are social interaction, social support, and higher self-efficacy.[211] These will help you connect more, receive more, and become more empowered. PTG is facilitated largely by social connections, as relief is found through talking about the trauma and growth following the event. It is in telling these stories to others that a new narrative is developed. Questions of purpose and meaning are reconstructed as emotional aspects of the events are revealed in an intimate connection. Survivors learn to believe in themselves again as they tell the story to those they trust.

The positivity effect seeks to help you thrive and optimally function. The goal is to find ways to attain and then maintain this positive outlook, positive emotions, and effectiveness. As you learned in the introduction, negative thoughts are like pebbles, and positive thoughts are like feathers. The work is meant to reduce negativity, increase positivity, and eventually make this shift sustainable. The framework for shifting that fulcrum point consists of strengthening core skills.

Each element of our exploration of hope, empowerment, resilience, and optimism has offered ways to key into emotional regulation by either upregulating the positive or downregulating the negative. In exploring PTG, you've learned how individuals, under the direst circumstances, make reliable change happen. But what does it mean to strengthen core skills, and how does it happen? One proven way to create endurable transformation is through your passion for a specific activity.[212]

Harnessing Harmonious Passion

Passion is a powerful positive emotion in our lives. But how does it work, and what can we do to get more of it? We can learn a lot from a group whose motivation and drive have been studied extensively.

Olympians cultivate passion in a way that science is only just beginning to understand. Studies reveal that passion is the essence of what makes Olympians (and anyone wishing to be successful) strive and succeed. We have learned from these athletes and other skilled performers that, when harnessed properly, passion makes us fully engaged with who we are—and what we are most capable of doing.

Bob Vallerand, at the University of Quebec in Montreal, has been researching passion for more than two decades and has won awards from the Olympic committee for his insights. He has been able to demonstrate how passion motivates and boosts an objective measure of performance.

Those who are passionate have a love of (or place a high value on) an object, concept, activity, or person that draws them deeply to invest time and energy. This means they are often thinking about and engaging in what they love to do—or whom they want to be with. It's so ingrained in their way of being that passionate engagement has become part of their identity. We become our passions.

Research shows that those with passion engage in deliberate practice, which is then a positive predictor of objective performance. This makes sense. If you are passionate about what you do, you deliberately do it more often, and in the sports world (as in the music world, and other professions and hobbies), the more you do something, the better you get.

Yet while passion may get you to the promised land of better performance, it comes in two forms: harmonious and obsessive. One will take a greater toll on you than the other. As the name implies, harmonious passion is in harmony with who you are, who you want to be, and doing and being what is true to yourself. It is autonomous, meaning that you can deeply engage and then stop, and it engages you very often, for several hours a week and often over many years. Harmonious passion is what you want, because when you're doing the things you love to do, you are completely absorbed in them, and it becomes a natural extension of your identity. When something is part of your identity, it taps into your self-esteem. You do it, and it makes you feel good about yourself, and the motivation comes from within. You are in alignment with who you are, what you want, and what you are doing. You are in flow, in an optimal state of functioning where time melts, and the activity has value on its own. Doing something you have a harmonious passion for fills you up—and keeps you going. This is the level of absorption and joy we want out of life.

Obsessive passion has a different feel to it—like the activity controls you and causes conflicts with the self and life. It is less adaptive and potentially more maladaptive. Obsessive passion is the type we have because of the payoff. We want to please someone, win the award, or get the money, the trophy, the raise, or the relationship. What makes obsessive passion troublesome is that it tends to interfere with our life. We might, indeed, succeed in the area we are obsessively passionate about but fail in other equally important and meaningful areas of life. There may be an uncontrollable urge to engage in the passion—often to the detriment of other important needs.

What Vallerand and his colleagues found is that the process of achievement is different depending on whether you are harmoniously or obsessively passionate.[213] Those who are harmonious use a coherent and focused mastery achievement process. This is an internally driven approach, and the deliberate practice comes from the desire to master the skill(s), leading to better objective performance. Such an approach is highly adaptive and promotes subjective well-being.

Those with obsessive passion often have a conflicted achievement process. While they too attempt to master the activity, they may also be driven by the maladaptive goals of trying to avoid failure and beat others.[214] The obsessively passionate workaholic neglects his family. The mother that works out seven days a week is often injured. The 16-year-old is holed up in their room playing video games when he should be studying for the midterm. People with obsessive passion do not have an off button.

Unless they are doing what they are passionate about, they don't feel right, and their self-concept and self-esteem suffer. Essentially, either you control your passion or your passion controls you. When the thing you do controls you, it is an obsessive passion. When you can step away from it and yet give it your all when you are engaged toward mastery, it is harmonious.

Not surprisingly, recent research[215] has shown a relationship between psychological capital, harmonious passion, and one's self-esteem and identity. Those with high psychological capital are internally driven and harmoniously passionate. They have higher self-esteem, which makes them flexible and adaptable around achieving goals. The interventions you've been exploring can help support the kind of passion you want in your life.

Keeping in mind our pebbles-and-feathers scale, the fulcrum point moves as a result of having more harmonious passion. The question then becomes, what is it that makes harmonious passion happen, and how does that help generate more positive emotions? Alternatively, what is it that causes an obsessive passion to arise and generate negative emotions? New research finds that depending on the type of passion, the increase of positive emotions or negative emotions comes from something you are already familiar with—how you appraise the situation.[216]

Remember back in chapter 4 when we explored threat appraisal? When you perceive something as a threat, this reduces the kinds of responses you have. Typically, this type of appraisal induces fear and limits your emotional reactions to fight, flight, or freeze. We also noted this in chapter 5 when exploring the difference between pessimists and optimists. The pessimists, as you may remember, will use threat appraisal as well, leading to negative emotions. So it is too with obsessive passion. Those with obsessive passion are operating under a threat appraisal—the fear of failure and not winning.

Harmonious passion is more likely to be found in those with high resilience and optimism—and those with PTG—in making a challenge appraisal rather than one of a threat. The challenge appraisal happens when a demand is evaluated as a positive opportunity to control or respond to a difficult demand. Through a challenge appraisal, harmonious passion feeds our positive emotions while providing the ability to respond to ongoing difficulties. This is exactly what Steve Jobs meant when he said, "It [what you choose to do] has got to be something that you're passionate about, because otherwise you won't have the perseverance to see it through."

EXPLORATION: Choosing Your Passion

What do you love to do? Let's explore what type of passions are already in your life. Use your journal to write down your reflections to this prompt.

Write about a favorite activity that deeply draws your engagement. Recall everything you can about the experience and include as much detail as possible—almost as if you are reliving it. Pay particular attention to what it feels like when you're engaged with it, and also what it's like for you to stop and break away. Here are some questions for you to ask yourself as you reflect on your answer.

1. Does my mood depend on being able to do the activity?

2. Does the activity reflect the qualities I like about myself?

3. Is my need to do the activity hard to control?

4. Do I keep finding new things with the activity that make me appreciate it more?

5. Does it feel like I cannot live without it?

6. Does it allow me to live a variety of experiences?

What did you learn about the activity you chose to write about? Repeat this with other activities and see what your reflections are. The obsessive-passion people would probably answer the *odd* number questions with a *yes*. The harmoniously passionate likely answer the *even* ones with a yes.

If your passions seem more obsessive, try these approaches scientists recommend[217] to help break the grip of the threat appraisal and urge.

1. *Take a break.* Schedule time away from the activity and plan it out ahead of time. In your journal, talk about how this transition felt and what might make it easier to do.

2. *Leave work at work.* If you feel obsessively passionate, leave your work at work. Make time for your phone to be off and your emails unanswered. If you don't make time for yourself, the crush of the demand will make work activate a threat response.

3. *Change your thinking.* Deliberately change your thoughts from *must* and *need* (obsessive-passion thinking) to *want* and *desire,* harmonious-passion thoughts. Research shows this deliberate intention has the potential to increase harmonious passion and self-esteem.[218].

4. *Try something new.* See if there's anything else that can pique your interest and engagement. This may provide some relief and may even kindle harmonious passion.

I've included this work on passion because the research indicates that the cognitive and emotional features of PTG are facilitated by passion—both kinds.[219] This is important to know because passionate activity, obsessive or harmonious, can help pull you out and through. It allows you to invest in that dialectical process of holding two opposite truths—the pain caused by the traumatic event, and the investment in passion. Being obsessively passionate is better than not being passionate at all.

Yet our focus here is on striving toward harmonious passion, because it results in more positivity and less worry, whereas obsessive passion is linked to greater negativity and worry.[220] Passion is important for enhanced well-being following PTG. *Harmonious* passion makes this journey a joyful one.

Now that you are tipping the scale in favor of positivity, let's look at how we can bring all these explorations and theories together in our final chapter.

CHAPTER 7

Be Ready for a Life of Thriving

*I urge you to please notice when you are happy, and exclaim or murmur
or think at some point, "If this isn't nice, I don't know what is."*

—Kurt Vonnegut

When I went through great difficulties in my life, it prompted a deep look
into the science of positivity and its application. The result was a transformation in how I thought, felt, and acted in the world—I changed radically and permanently. Not overnight, but over time I grew, evolved, and
leaned into the future in a way that I never had before. There was—and
is—a new source of energy, a deeper vision of what is possible, and a fero-
cious appetite for wanting to help inspire others to find the courage to
make the change.

I hope you are feeling some of this too. For me, a spark ignited inside
to bring about this change. Hopefully, as you feel the shift and transform
from the inside, the desire to help and be part of others' transformation
will help too. As Thich Nhat Hanh reminded us, "The way out is in."

I wrote this book to offer three things. The first is to introduce you to
the new science of hope and update you on the tremendous advances in
the science and application of empowerment, resilience, and optimism.
The second is to provide explorations designed to take the research and
put it into action. This can give you experiences to help shift your perceptions while regulating emotions. If you've made it this far and have been
doing the exercises along the way, perhaps you have already started to feel
the significance of the positivity effect. I hope so.

The third thing the positivity effect offers is preparedness. This provides a platform for change by creating ongoing positive transformations so you experience a new reality. You need to cultivate a readiness for good things to happen. Then you will be on full alert for what's to come.

Readiness arrives at the very end of training. Whether in sports, music, firefighting, flying an airplane, becoming a branch manager, getting your driver's license, having a gallery opening, or becoming a therapist, you get trained—you get prepared. This last chapter is devoted to having the forethought to effectively meet what appears.

The positivity effect gets you prepared for a good life. Not a life void of struggle, pain, and sorrow, but one filled with the wholeheartedness needed to cope with and evolve from these difficulties. I've been in the very fortunate position to watch people transform, and stay changed. While preparing people to learn how to take control of improving their life, I've witnessed firsthand thousands of students transform in my Positive Psychology and The Healing Power of Hope courses and spoken to thousands more on these principles. After classes, talks, or workshops, I ask them for their top takeaway for putting positivity into practice, to get ready for a happier life. I am anticipating that some of these responses might be similar to yours. Here are just a few important takeaways people have had.

1. Move toward, not away from, conflict.

2. Immediately challenge negative thinking that repeats itself.

3. Rumination is like a mosquito bite that has the potential to infect you. Stop the bite before it happens. Think of the beginning ruminating thought like the buzzing sound of a mosquito getting close. It will be in your best interest to swat it away and put on repellant.

4. See ambivalence, uncertainty, and negativity as allies to help you grow—not obstacles designed to defeat you.

5. Find ways to harvest as much positivity in your life as you can.

6. Joy is all around us, and learning to look for it will facilitate more of it coming your way.

7. Remember the positive, extraordinary, and loving moments in your life and use them when the going gets tough.

8. Live in your strength.

9. Do what makes you happy and help others do the same.

10. Live the golden and silver rules. Do unto others what you'd want them to do to you—and don't do to them what you wouldn't want them doing to you.

11. Peace in the world starts with peace in your heart.

12. Circumstance doesn't define me—it reveals me [from James Allen].

13. Sometimes doing nothing requires great effort.

14. The agitation I feel from a difficult situation is a call to action.

15. I'm not meant to be happy all the time, but I'm not meant to be chronically miserable either.

16. If you have a choice between smiling and frowning, pick the one you want to be remembered by.

17. I'd rather be a ray of sunshine than a dark cloud in someone's life.

18. Be around those who inspire, not expire you.

19. *Love* and *hope* are verbs.

20. Self-compassion is being kind to yourself so you can be kind to others.

The chapters preceding this one had a specific plan and outline to them that were designed to be layered and cumulative. We moved from simple ideas, like the pebbles and feathers, to more complex responses and processes, such as post-traumatic growth and harmonious passion. The exercises moved from the outside, noticing the peace and joy around you, to the inside, where you were asked to hold on to difficult feelings. Each exploration was part of a set of skills needed to get ready. You've gone from wax on, wax off, to the final rounds of the championship.

Yet, what I know about how true change takes place is that it isn't easy. We are changing habits of thought, feelings, and behavior, and this means we can expect some pushback from our nervous system and our mind. Let me give you an example.

EXPLORATION: Facilitating Change

Hold your hands out in front of you, elbows locked, with your thumbs about an inch from each other and your fingers spread apart. Now shake your hands, as if you were waving with both of them at someone, trying to get their attention. Then...slow up the one on the left.

Stay with this process and note what happens. In the beginning, there is some confusion and a bit of a struggle. It is hard to make your left hand do something different than your right. But if you keep trying, something magical may happen. You may become able to do this with very little effort.

Please write down your experience in your journal. What was it like to begin trying to regulate, see some success, and then master it? Within about two minutes, many people can do it. What was your experience?

This exploration shows how the nervous system is organized and designed to respond unilaterally to a novel stimulus. This means that when we are challenged with something new, we don't know how to have a refined response. Yet our consciousness, attention, and feedback give us a way to regulate our progress and get control over it.

If you take a minute or two to practice, you may see that by focusing your attention on a specific intention—to slow up the hand on the left—you can focus your awareness and have a different response. You might just master self-regulation by attending to a goal with great specificity.

This is exactly what you are doing by learning the positivity effect—directing your attention toward the purpose of emotional self-regulation. Each lesson brought a new challenge. Then, what you originally had to think about so diligently may have become second-nature.

I can easily slow up my left hand—because I have practiced. I'm ready. As you get ready to bring your change out into the world, you are going to be ready too.

Surfing with Your New Skills

The six chapters you've completed involved a set of skills and principles designed to build upon each other. They were not randomly constructed, but rather, represent a structure that supports how transformation happens, based on science and experience. Since the chapters were organized based on both awareness and skill development needed to awaken the positivity effect, this is a good place to review the principles and abilities each section was meant to offer.

If you have ever tried surfing, you will have an idea of how the lessons and principles are ordered. The skills to get the surfboard up to speed to catch a wave are completely different from the skills needed to bounce up on the board and ride it. In the beginning, surfing is about lying flat on the board, swimming out beyond where the waves break, learning to sit and balance, turn, and orient the board, and then timing your paddling to get up to the speed of the wave.

Once that happens, the skill set changes. You now have to bounce up on the board, find your balance, and catch the edge of the wave to get a ride. Finally, you have to learn how to kick out when the wave comes into shore or loses its vitality, and get yourself back out beyond where the waves break—to *get ready* again.

The organization of the chapters in this book are like learning to surf. As you prepare to go out on your own, to be ready, let's briefly review the journey you've taken and the different skill sets you have learned.

As we began this book, we looked at the landscape and current state of the science aimed at mental health and well-being. We defined the problem, noting that while gains have been made through various treatment options designed to reduce negative symptoms, relapse rates demonstrate that these treatments do not last. The best antianxiety and antidepressant medicines, and the most effective psychotherapies aimed at reducing negative thinking, fail at least half the time.

Research shows that when combined with efforts to decrease symptoms, increasing positive emotions can help prevent relapse. Some of the most effective positive interventions come from the elements collectively known as *psychological capital* (psycap)—hope, empowerment, resilience, and optimism (HERO). These traits are up against recurring negative thoughts. The solution offered by the positivity effect is to take the best we have in psychotherapy and medicine to date and add another known approach.

When trying to tip the scale in favor of having fewer negatives and more positives in our thinking, I offered the analogy of pebbles to feathers, to represent the fact that (due to the negativity bias), negative thoughts have more weight to them than positive ones do. The ways to make this scale tip were detailed in the chapters on hope, empowerment, resilience, and optimism.

In chapter 1, you learned that changing your perception is central to becoming aware of more positivity—and this requires developing new habits of seeing. To tip the scale in favor of more positive emotions in your life, you need to add many more feathers, reduce the number of pebbles, and move the fulcrum point in positivity's favor by strengthening your core skills in these new habits.

To begin this process, we explored the existing balance of negative to positive thoughts in your mind. This let you assess the ratio of positive to negative thinking that you bring to the job of changing perception. The exercise of noticing the peace and joy around you allowed the memory of positivity to be triggered—adding to the positive emotions you experienced. You were encouraged to practice these perceptual and emotional skills in the same way the wax on/wax off practice developed muscle memory in The Karate Kid. Shifting perception is a basic skill. It is like learning to get you and your surfboard out beyond the wave break.

Chapter 2 introduced the first element of psycap—hope—as the only positive emotion that requires uncertainty or negativity to be activated. Hope is different from optimism and faith, as hope is the belief that a positive future outcome is possible, combined with a desire for that outcome. Optimism is a general sense that the future is going to be okay (not that you'll have control), and faith is the belief that something greater than you influences the future.

The intolerance of uncertainty (the tendency to react negatively to uncertain situations) is a primary cause of anxiety and rumination. It is also an opportunity for the uncertainty and our interpretation of it to intersect. This is where meaning is made and is influenced by the perceptual set—where what we see is a matter of our readiness to see it in a particular way.

This part is like learning to watch for good waves that have potential. You are making a decision about the intersection between the wave and your skill. Too large of a wave mixed with too little skill can be devastating. To demonstrate this, the symbol *13* was shown in two different contexts, interpreted differently depending on the set it was in.

Destructive rumination comes from uncertainty. So being able to see your unsureness through a different perceptual set allows you to tolerate uncertainty and generate less anxiety—less rumination. When you can align your skill and reduced anxiety with an attainable goal, you shift the destructive force of rumination into an aligned motivation. Your coping capacity will develop as you experience how your perception affects your mood and your mood changes your perception. For better or worse, mood and perspective will shift your perception. A surfer judges a wave not by deeming it good or bad, but by looking at the skill level it would take to surf it.

With the positivity effect, when you stop rumination from getting worse, it facilitates the expectation that the future will be better. This stops the negative mood from affecting your perception and allows a more positive one to take its place. Because you've done something you believe will directly help control the future, you are more likely to have hope. A skilled surfer sees the potential in the wave, not only the fear it could generate. You can change how you think.

Chapter 3 looked at empowerment, confidence, and perception. You learned about the default network with the idea that your brain works like a search engine. You have to be specific about what you are looking for; otherwise, it will guess at what we want, and the guess is often based on what is most available. We have to ensure that the brain is searching for specificity and positivity—your day can be seen as great or miserable depending on how you search for the answer.

After a storm, the skilled surfer goes out into the water, but the novice isn't confident. When you ruminate, the default network gets stuck in a loop that keeps you focused on the present, turning over your own auto-biographical information. Instead, you can feel empowered because you now know how to flip the switch and focus on the future—not marinate in the past and present.

Good surfers get better when they try more challenging waves, and this motto supports that: *I believe, therefore I achieve, and I achieve, therefore I believe.* This allows you to use the dynamics of reciprocity to build confidence and empowerment. To make something achievable, you must believe it is possible. Once it has been achieved, it supports the feeling that it can be done again.

There is continuity to confidence: achieving something believed possible strengthens confidence.

When our effort has an effect, the effect supports the effort. This is most obvious and evident with self-care. When you take care of your own needs, it feels good—which reinforces taking care of your own needs and teaches you to be confident and empowered. You can build confidence through positivity, by directing your thoughts away from the negative and toward more positive, loving thoughts—as in the case of loving-kindness meditation. When you think about or interact with those you have loving and positive feelings for, it creates positivity resonance—as with surfers who remember the successful waves they've ridden.

Through chapter 4, we explored the fact that you can imagine future possibilities, potentialities, and pitfalls. This is perhaps the most dynamic and constructive nature of your consciousness and is essential in being able to choose how you respond. It is at the heart of resilience. You don't just imagine what is already there— when your expectations are blocked, you generate and evaluate alternate possibilities. Your mind is like a GPS unit that looks for alternatives when there is an obstacle.

The surfer is aware of others in the water and makes adjustments. This reappraisal of the situation informs your capacity for dealing with setbacks through two essential features: how well you have dealt with various setbacks in the past, and the adaptability of your thinking—or what might be called *flexible self-regulation*.

When you are blocked from your expectations, the disequilibrium initiates equilibrium through self-regulation. Your awareness allows for reappraisal, and for new choices to be acted on. You don't just bounce back, but you bounce forward when your resilience uses a flexible mindset. The surfer adjusts their balance to continue using the energy of the wave while working around potential obstacles. This chapter taught you how to respond resiliently by using a mindful pause (an assessment) and cultivating a flexible mindset.

In chapter 5, we took a more detailed look at how optimism can allow you to borrow positive emotions from the future. Your interview with the Best Possible Self allowed you to directly encounter the feelings and wisdom of who you'd like to become. In addition, the differences between optimism and pessimism—recalling permanence, personal, and pervasive dimensions—gave you an insight into how optimists not only explain what has happened to them but also think about what's to come. Tragic optimism reveals how you can cultivate an optimistic mindset—particularly in difficult times and circumstances. Hearing there's a hurricane offshore prompts the skilled surfer to get their wetsuit out and ready their board for the next day.

Chapter 6 inspired you to tip the scales in favor of positivity in an ongoing way. You can make the shift to developing core skills, to ensure the sustainability of good feelings. With positivity, you will act in ways that not only help to regulate and balance the scales, but also keep them tipped in favor of more positivity. Surfers keep challenging themselves by trying again if they are unsuccessful, observing the skills of others, and learning from their past successes and failures.

With the WOOP technique, you focused on strategies to deal with obstacles in the path of goals. This approach allowed you to use more of the elements of psychological capital in combination, making their impact stronger in the regulation of your emotions. Through post-traumatic growth (PTG), you learned that exposure to a potentially traumatic event causes some people to have setbacks. For others, the event catapults them into thinking about the future and how they can adjust to the event going forward. Disastrous events can help you develop a greater appreciation for life, more gratitude, and warmer, more intimate relationships, with a greater sense of personal strength.

Through these explorations, you learned how to hold difficult feelings and not be overwhelmed by them; goodness and growth can come from having to face them. For PTG, you can use dialectical thinking to hold together in awareness two polar-opposite thoughts (like vulnerability and strength).

With harmonious passion as a motivator, an internally driven approach can enhance any effort. When you are not driven by the maladaptive goal of trying to avoid failure and beat others (obsessive passion), and you employ deliberate practice to master a skill, you have better objective performance. Such an approach is highly adaptive and promotes subjective well-being. Good surfers accept the challenges the waves and conditions present. You explored your passions and learned how to promote harmonious passion.

Now, in this chapter, you will explore how to be ready for the unknown. This is when you plan regular trips with your surfboard to new destinations.

Applying Your HERO Toolbox

Some interesting new research tells us something we intuitively know: Happy people smile and act playful, have a cheerful disposition, enjoy more positive emotions, and savor and reflect on their good fortune. The unhappy among us express criticism, feel and display guilt, and often seem irritated.[221] No wonder most of us like to be around happy people more.

If there is a desired personal evolution you are looking for, here is a chart offering the elements of psychological capital that can help. This chart highlights the connection between the thinking habit and its desired effect. You can use this chart not only in a *descriptive* way (describing what thinking habit has the potential to yield the desired effect) but also in a *prescriptive* way (when you want a desired effect, choosing which thinking habit you need to adopt).

Psychological Capital	Thinking Habit	Desired Effect
Hope	*Choose* to believe in control of the *future*	Agency and Control
Empowerment	*Capitalize* on *past* successes	Confidence
Resilience	*Cultivate* a flexible mindset in the *present*	Readiness and Courage
Optimism	*Convert* how we explain the *past* and expect the *future*	Perspective and Certainty

At the very core of psychological capital is knowing what is needed in a way that makes the situation more positive. You can bring your HERO toolbox to the situation and be ready to use what is in it to shift the conditions in your favor. The following questions can help you reduce negative responses and increase positive ones.

- How can I find positivity in an initial setback?

- How can I be better prepared when times get tough?

- How do I deepen my positive emotions?

You now have the tools needed to change and will need to use them until you gain familiarity with their application. Someone who masters their skill learns the basics of their craft; then they elevate their skill until it is integrated into their identity. I hope, in a similar way, that the skills in *The Positivity Effect* become part of who and how you are in the world. As you see yourself as a more hopeful, empowered, resilient, and optimistic person, you'll be happier and inspire others to take their own journey.

Maintaining a Balanced Sense of Fear

When you are negative, your options vanish. The chief overriding emotion that promotes negativity is fear. Fear constricts, limits, and keeps you blind to options other than basic survival. It restricts what you focus on, limits your choices, and puts all your energy (fight, flight, or freeze) into lashing out, escaping, or shutting down. There is nothing that comes from the core emotion of fear that has to do with options broader than staying alive. Will you get through if you act in this way? Perhaps. Will you flourish and thrive? Definitely not.

Fear comes from a threat appraisal. Your observing, higher self is watching and making sure you are in balance. When the metaphorical tiger actually shows up (or we make the assessment that the tiger has shown up), the threat appraisal triggers the fear response. At that moment, the options become very, very limited. Do you attack, retreat, or play dead?

When the threat response is constantly being triggered, when you start operating from a place of fear as your default, the scales tip. At this point, you likely feel limited, stuck, and lacking hope, empowerment, resilience, and optimism. Fear is the enemy of psychological capital.

This feeling of fear that comes from feeling threatened has been wired into your body to protect against predators and predicaments. It is necessary to have the ability to accurately access the conditions, to stay alert to what could be a threat, and to fire up your defenses in response, which gives you the ability to take risks.

But what happens if your capacity to make good risk assessments isn't so great? What happens when you sense there is more danger in the world than there may actually be? Under a threat response, everything you do is aimed only at survival. This puts your body into a state of ongoing threat response, which over time takes its toll. This is because the emergency system you have for the occasional threat was designed to get you out of danger, not to support your way of living.

Have you ever had a flat tire and used the "donut" spare in your car? If so, you may have been warned not to use the donut as a replacement. It is designed only to get you out of trouble and is only a temporary fix. Once you get to a safe place, the impaired tire can be repaired or replaced.

Your threat response is like a spare tire in the trunk of your car. Threat responses are with you all the time, but should only be used in case of an emergency. They're designed to get you out of trouble, then returned to storage until needed again.

Carrying around a spare tire helps you to travel confidently. Being ready for an emergency gives you the confidence to take risks. Those with higher amounts of psychological capital pay attention to certain elements in their life. They look at things in a way that perceives the situation in their favor but doesn't ignore the difficulties confronting them. They feel prepared to handle them because they draw on their experiences that suggest they will be able to get through the current difficulty and succeed. They travel well because they have the emotional equivalent of a spare tire. By being aware of the potential difficulties, they prepare for success.

But if you interpret too many things as threats, you lose the ability to discern when a real threat needs your full response. This is why the need for emotional self-regulation becomes central to your well-being. If it is too easy for you to feel threatened, you may need to take the time to remind yourself that not everything is something to worry about, and that right alongside genuine concerns are important positive realities you can acknowledge and highlight.

If you perceive a threat as a challenge, you will have more options to choose from. As it happens, one of the best ways to enhance your capacity for psychological capital is to savor what has uplifted you.[222] When good things happen, make them last.

EXPLORATION: Beyond Gratitude—Savoring the Past

In chapter 3, I invited you to look at your day through the default network and then through a gratitude lens. Here, we are aiming for more than acknowledging and highlighting these experiences—we are going to savor them.

Each day is filled with demands and interruptions. Some of them might be related, some random, and some unforeseen. But the one thing we can be certain of is that each day provides us with a host of daily demands, many of which can set us back or provide obstacles.

Begin with yesterday and make a list of the demands you experienced. Here is mine as a sample.

1. My partner is sick and had to have an emergency procedure.

2. I have a writing deadline that will be hard to meet.

3. I have a virtual keynote that was moved during class time.

4. The shower is leaking onto the dining room table.

5. The car part I've waited a month for came in and was wrong.

6. I got a parking ticket.

7. I have a report due with another person that is ill, and I'll have to finish it.

Now start a new list, and for yesterday note your personal uplifts. Again, here is mine as a sample.

1. My partner came through the procedure easily and without complication.

2. I was invited to be on a popular podcast to talk about my writing.

3. My favorite TV show posted two new episodes.

4. I have absolutely no mechanical skills—yet I fixed a crack in an outdoor ornament.

5. An article I wrote months ago was finally published.

6. I engaged in a wonderful meditation that offered some insights.

Take each item on the second list and hold the feeling you had when you experienced it. There was a moment that uplifted you. Was it pride? Joy? Serenity? Deep appreciation? Contentment? Recall the moment and resonate with the feeling, holding on to it for as long as you can before moving on to the next feeling.

Following this, write a summary of the experience of savoring, and note what shifted for you. My paragraph looks like this:

Somehow the combined feelings generated while savoring left me feeling accomplished, proud, relieved, joyous, and appreciative. These lingering feelings seemed to eclipse the potential threats that took place that day, and I feel as if I'll be able to manage to deal with them as the days go forward.

As a daily practice, combine this savoring exercise with your daily gratitude list. Always begin with the daily demands and end with the daily uplifts. This practice changes your perspective because positivity has been identified, expanded, and given a more central role in your thinking. This starts to soften any potential overfocus on feeling threatened and turns the disruptions and setbacks into challenges. By recalling and savoring in this way, you fortify your capacity to appraise a difficult situation in a different way.

By using the past to understand what invigorates, motivates, and enlivens you, you grasp the prototype for your future success. The feelings that have enriched you previously are the seeds you need to plant for future growth. Just as every sunflower has the seeds for an endless proliferation of sunflowers, each positive experience carries the seeds of future well-being. If you want to get an idea of what will fill you up in the future, look at what has worked for you in the past. When good things come to you, and you take the time to let them affect you, the positive emotions are like well-planted seeds. In savoring this positivity, it is as though you are fertilizing, watering, and nurturing their growth. Savored positive emotions expand their influence and set the stage for a greater yield.[223]

To understand this process, consider how sunflower seeds are harvested. The beautifully radiant sunflower, the very symbol of exuberance, after a time begins to turn down and droop. As the flower's energy begins to fade, the backside turns yellow-brown, and the tiny petals surrounding the developing seeds dry up and fall off. This drying-out process exposes the mature seeds, which can then be harvested and planted, allowing the process to continue.

In a similar fashion, positive emotions, like sunflowers, are not designed to last. They are meant to bloom and flourish and then fade, exposing the seeds for the next crop of positivity. You now know where to look for the seeds of tomorrow's well-being—look to where you flourished and thrived. Where you have experienced the magnificence of joy and positivity. Within the recollection of these moments lies the great potential for your future.

GOING FORWARD: Rose Thorn Bud

I'd like to support the extraordinary work you've done throughout this book by offering one last technique designed to help keep the positivity effect front and center. I've used it for years in classes and workshops, and it helps keep our thoughts and perspectives in balance.

The *rose* is a positive experience, the *thorn* is a challenge, and the *bud* is something good on the horizon. This image highlights the fact that there's always a mix of things going on—some good, some difficult, and some with potential. It is this very balance that keeps us aware that good things are present, even when there are thorns.

At the end of the day, the week, or another regular interval, share with at least one other person your rose—a good thing that is happening. It may be a source of pride, accomplishment, acknowledgment, joy, or satisfaction. Describe the rose in detail, including the feelings that go along with it. The retelling is also an opportunity for savoring the experience. When the person or people you're engaging with share their own rose, show your interest by asking questions and being curious. Help them relive their rose experience so they also get to savor the positivity.

Then take turns talking about the thorn in your lives. What is happening, or happened, that is a challenge, and what strategies you are using to cope? When you are on the listening end of this, always ask if your partner wants feedback; don't take it upon yourself to offer unsolicited advice about what you think needs to be done in the situation. This is an opportunity for compassionate listening. When you are sharing your own thorns, let your partner know if you want advice about what can be done in the situation or if you prefer to just have them listen. When you express to your partner what you want, you have a much better chance of getting what you need.

Finally, talk about the buds—the good things that are to come. Savoring what is on the horizon extends the positive feelings from a future event back in time, and allows you to fill up in the moment. It also allows you to share that potential joy with your partner(s).

In the spirit of the positivity effect, this technique allows you to see the thorns in your life as challenges, not just obstacles, and adds the positive emotions that are present and coming into your life, to keep that scale tipped in the positive direction.

I hope good things in life come as a result of the work you've done here. As you move forward, my wish is that you have fewer pebbles in your life, and a truckload of feathers delivered daily.

Acknowledgments

From the time I was three, I wanted to be a writer. I thought it was such a magnificent life, and early on, I navigated my life to steer myself in that direction. There are many people who have helped along the way to create a nurturing, safe, and growth environment for me to realize that early dream. Each has provided inspiration and guidance. For this book, these folks have helped beyond measure. Each, in a different way, has improved my writing. I am also a better person for having them in my life.

I have been extremely lucky to have magnificent teachers—Marty Seligman, James Pawelski, Angela Duckworth, and Adam Grant—who awakened my psychological curiosity and desire to write. They have all led by being exemplars of the highest caliber. I have also been fortunate to connect with Scott Barry Kaufman, Ryan Niemiec, Karen Whalen Berry, Bob McGrath, Tayyab Rashid, and Steve Leventhal. They are a unique brand of applied researchers who make positive psychology come alive. All of these teachers and influencers are magnificent human beings who, through their skill and kindness, have provided a vision and path for being a writer in the field of positive psychology. Chief among these is Dr. Lisa Miller, founder of the Spirituality Mind Body Institute at Teachers College, Columbia University, in New York City. Through her encouragement, support, and belief in me, she helped to awaken a spiritual, transcendent relationship within me. She sets the example for how such an awakening can be channeled into applying the science of spirituality and positive psychology.

The editorial staff at New Harbinger—from Wendy Millstine and Jennye Garibaldi, acquisitions editors, to Jennifer Holder, coordinating and developmental editor, and Caleb Beckwith and Teja Watson—have been extraordinary. At every turn, their encouragement, suggestions, and concerns have improved my writing and given substance and flow to my ideas. They are dedicated guardians of the craft of writing—and I am very lucky to have them on my team.

Finally, there are those closest to me. Joel and Marilyn Morgovsky —lifelong friends whose presence remains a constant treasure. Jennifer Cory and Rocco Morrongiello, the dearest of friends, have become neighbors while I was writing this book. They can now have a break from me showing up on their doorstep with yet another idea or chapter draft of *The Positivity Effect*.

My daughter, Dr. Devon Tomasulo, is an instigator of creativity and a fountain of encouragement. She and my dear son-in-law, Spencer Fetrow, have their hands full right now, both with full-time jobs and two children under four. But they still make time for "Papa" to be with or FaceTime with Cal, my first grandson, and now Josephine, my first granddaughter— to whom this book is dedicated. It will be up to Jo and Cal's generation to continue finding new and creative ways to add to *The Positivity Effect*.

My love, muse, and partner, Andrea Szucs, is a daily outpouring of creative ideas and affirmations. As a therapist, professional actress, and professor, Andrea provides the very environment and loving atmosphere needed to blend science and creativity. I can only hope to provide the love and positivity for her that she has offered me.

Endnotes

Chapter 1

1   Kassebaum, N. J., M. Arora, R. M. Barber, J. Brown, & A. Roy.
    2016. "Global, Regional, and National Disability-Adjusted
    Life-Years (D.A.L.Y.S) for 315 Diseases and Injuries and Healthy
    Life Expectancy (HALE), 1990–2015: A Systematic Analysis for
    the Global Burden of Disease Study 2015." *The Lancet* 388(10053):
    1603–1658.

2   Anxiety and Depression Association of America. n.d.
    "Anxiety Disorders—Facts & Statistics." Accessed November 13,
    2022. https://adaa.org/understanding-anxiety/facts-statistics.

3   Anxiety and Depression Association of America. "Anxiety
    Disorders—Facts & Statistics."

4   Anxiety and Depression Association of America. "Anxiety
    Disorders—Facts & Statistics.

5   Dibdin, E. 2021. "9 Unusual Anxiety Symptoms You Might Not
    Know About," *Psych Central*, July 6, 2021. https://psychcentral
    .com/anxiety/unusual-anxiety-symptoms-you-might-not-know-about.

6   Wallis, K. A., M. Donald, & J. Moncrieff. 2021. "Antidepressant
    Prescribing in General Practice: A Call to Action." *Australian
    Journal of General Practice* 50(12): 954–956.

7   Takayanagi, Y., A. P. Spira, O. J. Bienvenu, R. S. Hock, M. C.
    Carras, W. W. Eaton, et al. 2014. "Antidepressant Use
    and Lifetime History of Mental Disorders in a Community Sample:
    Results from the Baltimore Epidemiologic Catchment Area Study."
    The Journal of Clinical Psychiatry 76(1): 40–44.

8   Kirsch, Irving. 2019. "Placebo Effect in the Treatment of Depression and Anxiety." *Frontiers in Psychiatry* 10: 407.

9   Wallis, Donald, & Moncrieff. "Antidepressant Prescribing in General Practice."

10   Longo, L. P., & B. Johnson. 2000. "Addiction: Part I. Benzodiazepines—Side Effects, Abuse Risk, and Alternatives." *American Family Physician* 61(7): 2121.

11   McLaughlin, M. n.d. "Anxiety and Depression: Why Don't We Want to Take Medication?" *Heartgrove Behavioral Health System.* Accessed November 13, 2022. https://www.hartgrove hospital.com/anxiety-depression-dont-want-take-medication.

12   Chekroud, A. M., D. Foster, A. B. Zheutlin, D. M. Gerhard, B. Roy, N. Koutsouleris, & J. H. Krystal. 2018. "Predicting Barriers to Treatment for Depression in a U.S. National Sample: A Cross-Sectional, Proof-of-Concept Study." *Psychiatric Services* 69(8): 927–934.

13   Levy, H. C., E. M. O'Bryan, & D. F. Tolin. 2021. "A Meta-Analysis of Relapse Rates in Cognitive-Behavioral Therapy for Anxiety Disorders." *Journal of Anxiety Disorders* 81: 102407.

14   Levy, H. C., K. T. Stevens, & D. F. Tolin. 2022. "Research Review: A Meta–Analysis of Relapse Rates in Cognitive Behavioral Therapy for Anxiety and Related Disorders in Youth." *Journal of Child Psychology and Psychiatry* 63(3): 252–260.

15   Ali, S., L. Rhodes, O. Moreea, D. McMillan, S. Gilbody, C. Leach, et al. 2017. "How Durable Is the Effect of Low-Intensity C.B.T. for Depression and Anxiety? Remission and Relapse in a Longitudinal Cohort Study." *Behaviour Research and Therapy* 94: 1–8.

16   Otto, M. W., R. K. McHugh, & K. M. Kantak. 2010. "Combined Pharmacotherapy and Cognitive-Behavioral Therapy for Anxiety Disorders: Medication Effects, Glucocorticoids, and Attenuated Treatment Outcomes." *Clinical Psychology: Science and Practice* 17(2): 91–103.

17 Lynch, D., K. R. Laws, & P. J. McKenna. 2010. "Cognitive Behavioural Therapy for Major Psychiatric Disorder: Does It Really Work? A Meta-Analytical Review of Well-Controlled Trials." *Psychological Medicine* 40(1): 9–24.

18 Levy, O'Bryan, & Tolin. "A Meta-Analysis of Relapse Rates in Cognitive-Behavioral Therapy for Anxiety Disorders."

19 Rashid, T., & M. K. A-H. Baddar. 2019. "Positive Psychotherapy: Clinical and Cross-Cultural Applications of Positive Psychology." In *Positive Psychology in the Middle East/North Africa*, edited by L. Lambert & N. Pasha-Zaidi. Springer Nature Switzerland.

20 Bahadur, N. 2020. "What Is Resilience, and Can It Help Us Bounce Back from This?" *Self*, May 28, 2020. https://www.self .com/story/what-is-resilience.

21 Nabizadeh, R., N. Ensanimehr, & S. Ehsani. 2019. "Investigating the Impact of the Achievement Motivation on Psychological Well-Being by Investigating the Mediating Role of Ego Strength and Psychological Capacity." *Razi Journal of Medical Sciences* 26(1): 68–77.

22 Luthans, F., K. W. Luthans, & B. C. Luthans. 2004. "Positive Psychological Capital: Beyond Human and Social Capital." *Business Horizons* 47(1): 45–50.

23 Luthans, F., & C. M. Youssef-Morgan. 2017. "Psychological Capital: An Evidence-Based Positive Approach." *Annual Review of Organizational Psychology and Organizational Behavior* 4: 339–366.

24 Luthans, Luthans, & Luthans. "Positive Psychological Capital."

25 Belil, F., F. Alhani, A. Ebadi, & A. Kazemnejad. 2018. "Self-Efficacy of People with Chronic Conditions: A Qualitative Directed Content Analysis." *Journal of Clinical Medicine* 7(11): 411.

26 Tseng, J., & J. Poppenk. 2020. "Brain Meta-State Transitions Demarcate Thoughts across Task Contexts Exposing the Mental Noise of Trait Neuroticism." *Nature Communications* 11(1): 1–12.

27 Harris, R. 2008. *The Happiness Trap: How to Stop Struggling and Start Living*. Boston: Trumpeter Books.

28 Cohn, M. A., B. L. Fredrickson, S. L. Brown, J. A. Mikels, & A. M. Conway. 2009. "Happiness Unpacked: Positive Emotions Increase Life Satisfaction by Building Resilience." *Emotion* 9(3): 361–368.

29 Veilleux, J. C., N. M. Lankford, M. A. Hill, K. D. Skinner, K. D. Chamberlain, D. E. Baker, et al. 2020. "Affect Balance Predicts Daily Emotional Experience." *Personality and Individual Differences* 154(109683).

30 Mochon, D., M. I. Norton, & D. Ariely. 2008. "Getting Off the Hedonic Treadmill, One Step at a Time: The Impact of Regular Religious Practice and Exercise on Well-Being." *Journal of Economic Psychology* 29(5): 632–642.

31 van Cappellen, P., E. L. Rice, L. I. Catalino, & B. L. Fredrickson. 2018. "Positive Affective Processes Underlie Positive Health Behavior Change." *Psychology & Health* 33(1): 77–97.

32 Quirin, M., R. C. Bode, & J. Kuhl. 2011. "Recovering from Negative Events by Boosting Implicit Positive Affect." *Cognition & Emotion* 25(3): 559–570.

Chapter 2

33 Valkov, P., & T. Stoeva. 2017. "The Role of Faith and Optimism in Coping with Stress." *Psychology–Theory & Practice* 3.

34 Dursun, P. 2021. "Optimism, Hope and Subjective Well-Being: A Literature Overview." *Çatalhöyük Uluslararası Turizm ve Sosyal Araştırmalar Dergisi* (6): 61–74.

35 Paul Victor, C. G., & J. V. Treschuk. 2020. "Critical Literature Review on the Definition Clarity of the Concept of Faith, Religion, and Spirituality." *Journal of Holistic Nursing* 38(1): 107–113.

36 Luo, S. X., F. Van Horen, K. Millet, & M. Zeelenberg. 2020. "What We Talk about When We Talk about Hope: A Prototype Analysis." *Emotion* 22(4): 751–768.

37 Huang, T. Y., V. Souitaris, & S. G. Barsade. 2019. "Which Matters More? Group Fear versus Hope in Entrepreneurial Escalation of Commitment." *Strategic Management Journal* 40(11): 1852–1881.

38 Tu, M., F. Wang, S. Shen, H. Wang, & J. Feng. 2021. "Influences of Psychological Intervention on Negative Emotion, Cancer-Related Fatigue, and Level of Hope in Lung Cancer Chemotherapy Patients Based on the Perma Framework." *Iranian Journal of Public Health* 50(4): 728–736.

39 Sieben, N. 2018. "Hope in Education." In *Writing Hope Strategies for Writing Success in Secondary Schools*. Boston: Brill Sense.

40 Cherrington, A. M. 2018. "Research as Hope-Intervention: Mobilising Hope in a South African Higher Education Context." *South African Journal of Education* 38(4): 1–9.

41 Freire, P. 2021. *Pedagogy of Hope: Reliving Pedagogy of the Oppressed*. London: Bloomsbury Publishing.

42 Munoz, R. T., S. Hoppes, C. M. Hellman, K. L. Brunk, J. E. Bragg, & C. Cummins. 2018. "The Effects of Mindfulness Meditation on Hope and Stress." *Research on Social Work Practice* 28(6): 696–707.

43 Madden, W., S. Green, & A. M. Grant. 2011. "A Pilot Study Evaluating Strengths-Based Coaching for Primary School Students: Enhancing Engagement and Hope." *International Coaching Psychology Review* 6(1): 71–83.

44 Cheavens, J. S., & M. M. Guter. 2018. "Hope Therapy." In *The Oxford Handbook of Hope*, edited by M. W. Gallagher & S. J. Lopez. New York: Oxford University Press.

45 van Zomeren, M., I. L. Pauls, & S. Cohen-Chen. 2019. "Is Hope Good for Motivating Collective Action in the Context of Climate Change? Differentiating Hope's Emotion-and Problem-Focused Coping Functions." *Global Environmental Change* 58: 101915.

46 Leontopoulou, S. 2020. "Hope Interventions for the Promotion of Well-Being Throughout the Life Cycle." In *Oxford Research Encyclopedia of Education*, edited by R. Papa. New York: Oxford University Press.

47 Gallagher, M. W., L. J. Long, & C. A. Phillips. 2020. "Hope, Optimism, Self-Efficacy, and Posttraumatic Stress Disorder: A Meta-Analytic Review of the Protective Effects of Positive Expectancies." *Journal of Clinical Psychology* 76(3): 329–355.

48 Luo, Van Horen, Millet, & Zeelenberg. "What We Talk about When We Talk about Hope: A Prototype Analysis."

49 Tomasulo, D. 2020. *Learned Hopefulness: The Power of Positivity to Overcome Depression*. Oakland, CA: New Harbinger Publications.

50 Landy, R. J. 1996. *Persona and Performance: The Meaning of Role in Drama, Therapy, and Everyday Life*. New York: Guilford Press.

51 Stein, M. B., & J. Sareen. 2015. "Generalized Anxiety Disorder." *New England Journal of Medicine* 373(21): 2059–2068.

52 Bomyea, J., H. J. Ramsawh, T. M. Ball, C. T. Taylor, M. P. Paulus, A. J. Lang, et al. 2015. "Intolerance of Uncertainty as a Mediator of Reductions in Worry in a Cognitive Behavioral Treatment Program for Generalized Anxiety Disorder." *Journal of Anxiety Disorders* 33: 90–94.

53 Gentes, E. L., & A. M. Ruscio. 2011. "A Meta-Analysis of the Relation of Intolerance of Uncertainty to Symptoms of Generalized Anxiety Disorder, Major Depressive Disorder, and Obsessive-Compulsive Disorder." *Clinical Psychology Review* 31: 923–933.

54 Bruner, J. S., & A. L. Minturn. 1955. "Perceptual Identification and Perceptual Organization." *Journal of General Psychology* 53: 21–28.

55 Watkins, E. R. 2008. "Constructive and Unconstructive Repetitive Thought." *Psychological Bulletin* 134(2): 163–206.

56 Watkins, E. R., & H. Roberts. 2020. "Reflecting on Rumination: Consequences, Causes, Mechanisms and Treatment of Rumination." *Behaviour Research and Therapy* 127: 103573.

57 Pérez-Fuentes, M. d. C., M. d. M. M. Jurado, Á. M. Martínez, & J. J. G. Linares. 2020. "Threat of COVID-19 and Emotional State during Quarantine: Positive and Negative Affect as Mediators in a Cross-Sectional Study of the Spanish Population." *PLOS ONE* 15(6): e0235305.

58 Algorani, E. B., & V. Gupta. 2022. "Coping Mechanisms." In *StatPearls*. Tampa, FL: StatPearls Publishing.

59 Fredrickson, B. L., & T. Joiner. 2018. "Reflections on Positive Emotions and Upward Spirals." *Perspectives on Psychological Science* 13(2): 194–199.

Chapter 3

60 Buckner, R. L., & L. M. DiNicola. 2019. "The Brain's Default Network: Updated Anatomy, Physiology and Evolving Insights." *Nature Reviews Neuroscience* 20(10): 593–608.

61 Kaiser, R. H., M. S. Kang, Y. Lew, J. Van Der Feen, B. Aguirre, R. Clegg, et al. 2019. "Abnormal Frontoinsular–Default Network Dynamics in Adolescent Depression and Rumination: A Preliminary Resting-State Co-activation Pattern Analysis." *Neuropsychopharmacology* 44(9): 1604–1612.

62 Reiss, S. 1991. "Expectancy Model of Fear, Anxiety, and Panic." *Clinical Psychology Review* 11(2): 141–153.

63 Duong, C. D. 2021. "The Impact of Fear and Anxiety of COVID-19 on Life Satisfaction: Psychological Distress and Sleep Disturbance as Mediators." *Personality and Individual Differences* 178: 110869.

64 Arslan, G., M. Yıldırım, A. Tanhan, M. Buluş, & K. A. Allen. 2021. "Coronavirus Stress, Optimism-Pessimism, Psychological Inflexibility, and Psychological Health: Psychometric Properties of the Coronavirus Stress Measure." *International Journal of Mental Health and Addiction* 19(6): 2423–2439.

65 Liu, J., W. Wang, Q. Hu, P. Wang, L. Lei, & S. Jiang. 2021. "The Relationship between Phubbing and the Depression of Primary and Secondary School Teachers: A Moderated Mediation Model of Rumination and Job Burnout." *Journal of Affective Disorders* 295: 498–504.

66 Buckner, R. L. 2013. "The Brain's Default Network: Origins and Implications for the Study of Psychosis." *Dialogues in Clinical Neuroscience* 15(3): 351–358.

67 Buckner. "The Brain's Default Network: Origins and Implications for the Study of Psychosis."

68 Portocarrero, F. F., K. Gonzalez, & M. Ekema-Agbaw. 2020. "A Meta-Analytic Review of the Relationship Between Dispositional Gratitude and Well-Being. *Personality and Individual Differences* 164: 110101.

69 Fredrickson, B. L. 2004. "Gratitude, Like Other Positive Emotions, Broadens and Builds." *The Psychology of Gratitude* 145: 166. New York: Oxford University Press.

70 Watkins, P. C., R. A. Emmons, & M. E. McCullough. 2004. "Gratitude and Subjective Well-Being." In *The Psychology of Gratitude*, edited by R. A. Emmons & M. E. McCullough. New York: Oxford University Press.

71 Watkins, Emmons, & McCullough. "Gratitude and Subjective Well-Being."

72 Wikipedia. n.d. "If You're Happy and You Know It." Last modified December 2022. https://en.wikipedia.org/wiki/If_You %27re_Happy_and_You_Know_It.

73 Honicke, T., & J. Broadbent. 2016. "The Influence of Academic Self-Efficacy on Academic Performance: A Systematic Review." *Educational Research Review* 17: 63–84.

74 Bandura, A. 1977. "Self-Efficacy: Toward a Unifying Theory of Behavioral Change." *Psychological Review* 84(2): 191–215.

75 Hsu, D. K., K. Burmeister-Lamp, S. A. Simmons, M. D. Foo, M. C. Hong, & J. D. Pipes. 2019. "'I Know I Can, but I Don't Fit': Perceived Fit, Self-Efficacy, and Entrepreneurial Intention." *Journal of Business Venturing* 34(2): 311–326.

76 Bender, A., & R. Ingram. 2018. "Connecting Attachment Style to Resilience: Contributions of Self-Care and Self-Efficacy." *Personality and Individual Differences* 130: 18–20.

77 Parks, S., M. D. Birtel, & R. J. Crisp. 2014. "Evidence That a Brief Meditation Exercise Can Reduce Prejudice toward Homeless People." *Social Psychology* 45: 458–465.

78 Johnson, D. P., D. L. Penn, B. L. Fredrickson, A. M. Kring, P. S. Meyer, L. I. Catalino, et al. 2011. "A Pilot Study of Loving-Kindness Meditation for the Negative Symptoms of Schizophrenia." *Schizophrenia Research* 129(23): 137–140.

79 Carson, J. W., F. J. Keefe, T. R. Lynch, K. M. Carson, V. Goli, A. M. Fras, et al. 2005. "Loving-Kindness Meditation for Chronic Low Back Pain Results from a Pilot Trial." *Journal of Holistic Nursing* 23(3): 287–304.

80 Schure, M. B., T. L. Simpson, M. Martinez, G. Sayre, & D. J. Kearney. 2018. "Mindfulness-Based Processes of Healing for Veterans with Post-Traumatic Stress Disorder." *The Journal of Alternative and Complementary Medicine* 24(11): 1063–1068.

81 Ratner, P. 2017. "Scientists Discover How Meditation Changes the Brain." *Big Think*, October 10, 2017. https://bigthink.com/paul-ratner/scientists-discover-how-meditation-changes-the-brain.

82 Roca, P., G. Diez, R. J. McNally, & C. Vazquez. 2021. "The Impact of Compassion Meditation Training on Psychological Variables: A Network Perspective." *Mindfulness* 12(4): 873–888.

83 Shahar, B., O. Szepsenwol, S. Zilcha-Mano, N. Haim, O. Zamir, S. Levi-Yeshuvi, et al. 2015. "A Wait-List Randomized Controlled Trial of Loving-Kindness Meditation Programme for Self-Criticism." *Clinical Psychology & Psychotherapy* 22(4): 346–356.

84 Danucalov, M. A., E. H. Kozasa, R. F. Afonso, J. C. Galduroz, & J. R. Leite. 2017. "Yoga and Compassion Meditation Program Improve Quality of Life and Self-Compassion in Family Caregivers of Alzheimer's Disease Patients: A Randomized Controlled Trial." *Geriatrics & Gerontology International* 17(1): 85–91.

85 Roca, Diez, McNally, & Vazquez. "The Impact of Compassion Meditation Training on Psychological Variables."

86 Fredrickson, B. L., & T. Joiner. 2018. "Reflections on Positive Emotions and Upward Spirals." *Perspectives on Psychological Science* 13(2): 194–199.

87 Fredrickson, B. L., A. J. Boulton, A. M. Firestine, P. Van Cappellen, S. B. Algoe, M. M. Brantley, et al. 2017. "Positive Emotion Correlates of Meditation Practice: A Comparison of Mindfulness Meditation and Loving-Kindness Meditation." *Mindfulness* 8(6): 1623–1633.

88 Fredrickson, B. L., M. A. Cohn, K. A. Coffey, J. Pek, & S. M. Finkel. 2008. "Open Hearts Build Lives: Positive Emotions, Induced through Loving-Kindness Meditation, Build Consequential Personal Resources." *Journal of Personality and Social Psychology* 95(5): 1045–1062.

89 Luberto, C. M., N. Shinday, R. Song, L. L. Philpotts, E. R. Park, G. L. Fricchione, et al. 2018. "A Systematic Review and Meta-Analysis of the Effects of Meditation on Empathy, Compassion, and Prosocial Behaviors." *Mindfulness* 9(3): 708–724.

90 Van Cappellen, P., L. I. Catalino, & B. L. Fredrickson. 2020. "A New Micro-Intervention to Increase the Enjoyment and Continued Practice of Meditation." *Emotion* 20(8): 1332–1343.

91 Major, B. C., K. D. Le Nguyen, K. B. Lundberg, & B. L. Fredrickson. 2018. "Well-Being Correlates of Perceived Positivity Resonance: Evidence from Trait and Episode-Level Assessments." *Personality and Social Psychology Bulletin* 44(12): 1631–1647.

92 Zhou, J., M. M. Prinzing, K. D. Le Nguyen, T. N. West, & B. L. Fredrickson. 2021. "The Goods in Everyday Love: Positivity Resonance Builds Prosociality." *Emotion* 22(1): 30–45.

93 Talsma, K., B. Schüz, R. Schwarzer, & K. Norris. 2018. "I Believe, Therefore, I Achieve (and Vice Versa): A Meta-Analytic Cross-Lagged Panel Analysis of Self-Efficacy and Academic Performance." *Learning and Individual Differences* 61: 136–150.

94 Fredrickson & Joiner. "Reflections on Positive Emotions and Upward Spirals."

95 Fredrickson & Joiner. "Reflections on Positive Emotions and Upward Spirals."

Chapter 4

96 Harms, P. D., L. Brady, D. Wood, & A. Silard. 2018. "Resilience and Well-Being." In *Handbook of Well-Being*, edited by E. Diener, S. Oishi, & L. Tay. Salt Lake City: DEF Publishers.

97 Kiken, L. G., & N. J. Shook. 2011. "Looking Up: Mindfulness Increases Positive Judgments and Reduces Negativity Bias." *Social Psychological and Personality Science* 2(4): 425–431.

98 Harms, Brady, Wood, & Silard. "Resilience and Well-Being."

99 Roepke, A. M., & M. E. Seligman. 2016. "Depression and Prospection." *British Journal of Clinical Psychology* 55(1): 23–48.

100 Seligman, M. E., P. Railton, R. F. Baumeister, & C. Sripada. 2013. "Navigating into the Future or Driven by the Past." *Perspectives on Psychological Science* 8(2): 119–141.

101 Baumeister, R. F., H. M. Maranges, & H. Sjåstad. 2018. "Consciousness of the Future as a Matrix of Maybe: Pragmatic Prospection and the Simulation of Alternative Possibilities." *Psychology of Consciousness: Theory, Research, and Practice* 5(3): 223–238.

102 Kiken & Shook. "Looking Up: Mindfulness Increases Positive Judgments and Reduces Negativity Bias."

103 Zandonella, C. 2017. "Brain's 'GPS' Does a Lot More than Just Navigate." Princeton University, March 30, 2017. https://www.princeton.edu/news/2017/03/30/brains-gps-does-lot-more-just-navigate.

104 Bonanno, G. A. 2021. "The Resilience Paradox." *European Journal of Psychotraumatology* 12(1): 1942642.

105 Captari, L. E., S. A. Riggs, & K. Stephen. 2021. "Attachment Processes Following Traumatic Loss: A Mediation Model Examining Identity Distress, Shattered Assumptions, Prolonged Grief, and Posttraumatic Growth." *Psychological Trauma: Theory, Research, Practice, and Policy* 13(1): 94–103.

106 Chopra, D. 2004. *The Spontaneous Fulfillment of Desire: Harnessing the Infinite Power of Coincidence.* New York: Harmony Books.

107 Labouvie-Vief, G. 2015. "Equilibrium and Disequilibrium in Development." In *Integrating Emotions and Cognition Throughout the Lifespan.* Switzerland: Springer International.

108 Bonanno, G. A. 2005. "Resilience in the Face of Potential Trauma." *Current Directions in Psychological Science* 14(3): 135–138.

109 Bonanno. "The Resilience Paradox."

110 Bonanno, G. A. 2021. *The End of Trauma: How the New Science of Resilience Changes How We Think About PTSD* (1st ed.). New York: Basic Books.

111 Bonanno. *The End of Trauma.*

112 Stevenson, J. C., A. Millings, & L. M. Emerson. 2019. "Psychological Well-Being and Coping: The Predictive Value of Adult Attachment, Dispositional Mindfulness, and Emotion Regulation." *Mindfulness* 10(2): 256–271.

113 Mohr, C., S. Braun, R. Bridler, F. Chmetz, J. P. Delfino, V. J. Kluckner, et al. 2014. "Insufficient Coping Behavior under Chronic Stress and Vulnerability to Psychiatric Disorders." *Psychopathology* 47(4): 235–243.

114 Kiken & Shook. "Looking Up: Mindfulness Increases Positive Judgments and Reduces Negativity Bias."

115 Stevenson, Millings, & Emerson. "Psychological Well-Being and Coping: The Predictive Value of Adult Attachment, Dispositional Mindfulness, and Emotion Regulation."

116 Ryan, R. M., & E. L. Deci. 2000. "Self-Determination Theory and the Facilitation of Intrinsic Motivation, Social Development, and Well-Being." *American Psychologist* 55(1): 68–78.

117 Bonanno. *The End of Trauma.*

118 Niemiec, R. 2016. "A Mindful Pause to Change Your Day." VIA Institute on Character, April, 25, 2016. https://www .viacharacter.org/topics/articles/a-mindful-pause-to-change-your -day#:~:text=How%20to%20Do%20a%20Mindful,I%20bring %20forward%20right%20now%3F.

119 Niemiec, R. M., & R. Pearce. 2021. "The Practice of Character Strengths: Unifying Definitions and Principles and Exploring What's Soaring, Emerging, and Ripe with Potential in Science and Practice." *Frontiers in Psychology* 11: 590220.

120 Tomasulo, D. 2020. *Learned Hopefulness: The Power of Positivity to Overcome Depression.* Oakland, CA: New Harbinger Publications.

121 Peterson, C., & M. E. Seligman. 2004. *Character Strengths and Virtues: A Handbook and Classification* (vol. 1). American Psychological Association; Oxford University Press.

122 https://www.viacharacter.org.

123 Ivtzan, I., R. M. Niemiec, & C. Briscoe. 2016. "A Study Investigating the Effects of Mindfulness-Based Strengths Practice (MBSP) on Well-Being." *International Journal of Wellbeing* 6(2): 1–13.

124 Bretherton, R., & R. M. Niemiec. 2019. "Mindfulness-Based Strengths Practice (MBSP)." In *Handbook of Mindfulness-Based Programmes*, edited by I. Ivtzan. Milton Park, UK: Routledge.

125 Whelan-Berry, K., & R. Niemiec. 2021. "Integrating Mindfulness and Character Strengths for Improved Well-Being, Stress, and Relationships: A Mixed-Methods Analysis of Mindfulness-Based Strengths Practice." *International Journal of Wellbeing* 11(1): 36–50.

Chapter 5

126 Scheier, M. F., & C. S. Carver. 2018. "Dispositional Optimism and Physical Health: A Long Look Back, a Quick Look Forward." *American Psychologist* 73(9): 1082–1094.

127 Rozanski, A., C. Bavishi, L. D. Kubzansky, & R. Cohen. 2019. "Association of Optimism with Cardiovascular Events and All-Cause Mortality: A Systematic Review and Meta-Analysis." *JAMA Network Open* 2(9): e1912200.

128 Eva, N., A. Newman, Z. Jiang, & M. Brouwer. 2020. "Career Optimism: A Systematic Review and Agenda for Future Research." *Journal of Vocational Behavior* 116(B): 103287.

129 Rand, K. L., M. L. Shanahan, I. C. Fischer, & S. K. Fortney. 2020. "Hope and Optimism as Predictors of Academic Performance and Subjective Well-Being in College Students." *Learning and Individual Differences* 81: 101906.

130 Rozanski, A., J. A. Blumenthal, K. W. Davidson, P. G. Saab, & L. Kubzansky. 2005. "The Epidemiology, Pathophysiology, and Management of Psychosocial Risk Factors in Cardiac Practice: The Emerging Field of Behavioral Cardiology." *Journal of the American College of Cardiology* 45(5): 637–651.

131 Duckworth, A. 2016. *Grit: The Power of Passion and Perseverance.* New York: Scribner.

132 Fredrickson, B. L., & T. Joiner. 2018. "Reflections on Positive Emotions and Upward Spirals." *Perspectives on Psychological Science* 13(2): 194–199.

133 Seligman, M. E. 2006. *Learned Optimism: How to Change Your Mind and Your Life.* New York: Vintage.

134 Carver, C. S., & M. F. Scheier. 2014. "Dispositional Optimism." *Trends in Cognitive Science* 18: 293–299.

135 Lee. L. O., P. James, E. S. Zevon, E. S. Kim, C. Trudel-Fitzgerald, A. Spiro III, et al. 2019. "Optimism is Associated with Exceptional Longevity in 2 Epidemiologic Cohorts of Men and Women." *Proceedings of the National Academy of Sciences* 116(37): 18357–18362.

136 Lee et al. "Optimism is Associated with Exceptional Longevity in 2 Epidemiologic Cohorts of Men and Women."

137 World Health Organization. 2020. "Healthy Ageing and Functional Ability." October 26, 2022. https://www.who.int /philippines/news/q-a-detail/healthy-ageing-and-functional-ability.

138 Miller, L., & J. V. Campo. 2021. "Depression in Adolescents." *New England Journal of Medicine*, 385(5): 445–449.

139 Weinberger, A. H., M. Gbedemah, A. M. Martinez, D. Nash, S. Galea, & R. D. Goodwin. 2018. "Trends in Depression Prevalence in the USA from 2005 to 2015: Widening Disparities in Vulnerable Groups." *Psychological Medicine* 48(8): 1308–1315.

140 Glenn, C. R., E. M. Kleiman, J. Kellerman, O. Pollak, C. B. Cha, E. C. Esposito, et al. 2020. "Annual Research Review: A Meta-Analytic Review of Worldwide Suicide Rates in Adolescents." *Journal of Child Psychology and Psychiatry* 61(3): 294–330.

141 Heekerens, J. B., & M. Eid. 2021. "Inducing Positive Affect and Positive Future Expectations Using the Best-Possible-Self Intervention: A Systematic Review and Meta-Analysis." *The Journal of Positive Psychology* 16(3): 322–347.

142 Loveday, P. M., G. P. Lovell, & C. M. Jones. 2018. "The Best Possible Selves Intervention: A Review of the Literature to Evaluate Efficacy and Guide Future Research." *Journal of Happiness Studies* 19: 607–628.

143 Layous, K., S. K. Nelson, & S. Lyubomirsky. 2013. "What Is the Optimal Way to Deliver a Positive Activity Intervention? The Case of Writing about One's Best Possible Selves." *Journal of Happiness Studies*, 14(2), 635–654.

144 Meevissen, Y. M., M. L. Peters, & H. J. Alberts. 2011. "Become More Optimistic by Imagining a Best Possible Self: Effects of a Two-Week Intervention." *Journal of Behavior Therapy and Experimental Psychiatry* 42(3): 371–378.

145 King, L. A. 2001. "The Health Benefits of Writing about Life Goals." *Personality and Social Psychology Bulletin* 27(7): 798–807.

146 Carrillo A., M. Martínez-Sanchis, E. Etchemendy, & R. M. Baños. 2019. "Qualitative Analysis of the Best Possible Self Intervention: Underlying Mechanisms That Influence Its Efficacy." *PLOS ONE* 14(5): e0216896.

147 Frattaroli, J. 2006. "Experimental Disclosure and Its Moderators: A Meta-Analysis." *Psychological Bulletin Journal* 132(6): 823–865.

148 Loveday, Lovell, & Jones. "The Best Possible Selves Intervention."

149 Meevissen, Peters, & Alberts. "Become More Optimistic by Imagining a Best Possible Self."

150 Loveday, Lovell, & Jones. "The Best Possible Selves Intervention."

151 Carillo, Martínez-Sanchez, Etchemendy, & Baños. "Qualitative Analysis of the Best Possible Self Intervention."

152 Seligman, M. E., P. R. Verkuil, & T. H. Kang. 2005. "Why Lawyers Are Unhappy." *Deakin Law Review* 10(1): 49–66.

153 Shapcott, S., S. David, & L. Hanson. 2017. "The Jury Is In: Law Schools Foster Students' Fixed Mindsets." *Law & Psychology Review* 42: 1–50.

154 Krill, P. R., R. Johnson, & L. Albert. 2016. "The Prevalence of Substance Use and Other Mental Health Concerns Among American Attorneys." *Journal of Addiction Medicine* 10(1): 46–52.

155 Anzalone, F. M. 2018. "Lawyer and Law Student Well-Being." *AALL Spectrum* 22(4): 44–46.

156 Oehme, K., & N. Stern. 2019. "Improving Lawyers' Health by Addressing the Impact of Adverse Childhood Experiences." *University of Richmond Law Review* 53: 1311–1338.

157 Sendroiu, I., L. Upenieks, & M. H. Schafer. 2021. "The Divergent Mental Health Effects of Dashed Expectations and Unfulfilled Aspirations: Evidence from American Lawyers' Careers." *Social Psychology Quarterly* 84(4): 376–397.

158 Sendroiu, Upenieks, & Schafer. "The Divergent Mental Health Effects of Dashed Expectations and Unfulfilled Aspirations."

159 The Nobel Prize. n.d. "The Nobel Prize in Physiology or Medicine 2009." https://www.nobelprize.org/prizes/medicine/2009/summary.

160 Puterman, E., & E. Epel. 2012. "An Intricate Dance: Life Experience, Multisystem Resiliency, and Rate of Telomere Decline throughout the Lifespan." *Social and Personality Psychology Compass* 6(11): 807–825.

161 Long, K. N., E. S. Kim, Y. Chen, M. F. Wilson, E. Worthington Jr., & T. J. VanderWeele. 2020. "The Role of Hope in Subsequent Health and Well-Being for Older Adults: An Outcome-Wide Longitudinal Approach." *Global Epidemiology* 2: 100018.

162 Warner, L. M. & R. Schwarzer. 2020. "Self-Efficacy and Health." In *The Wiley Encyclopedia of Health Psychology: Volume II, The Social Bases of Health Behavior* edited by K. Sweeny, M. L. Robbins, & L. M. Cohen. New York: Wiley-Blackwell.

163 Zeng, Y., & K. Shen. 2010. "Resilience Significantly Contributes to Exceptional Longevity." *Current Gerontology and Geriatrics Research* 2010: 525693.

164 Laranjeira, C., & A. Querido. 2022. "Hope and Optimism as an Opportunity to Improve the 'Positive Mental Health' Demand." *Frontiers in Psychology* 13: 827320.

165 Harvanek, Z. M., N. Fogelman, K. Xu, & R. Sinha. 2021. "Psychological and Biological Resilience Modulates the Effects of Stress on Epigenetic Aging." *Translational Psychiatry* 11(1): 1–9.

166 Mason, A. E., J. M. Adler, E. Puterman, A. Lakmazaheri, M. Brucker, K. Aschbacher, et al. 2019. "Stress Resilience: Narrative Identity May Buffer the Longitudinal Effects of Chronic Caregiving Stress on Mental Health and Telomere Shortening." *Brain, Behavior, and Immunity* 77: 101–109.

167 Hodes, R. J. 1999. "Telomere Length, Aging, and Somatic Cell Turnover." *Journal of Experimental Medicine* 190(2): 153–156.

168 Drury, S. S. 2021. "Building Resilience for Generations: The Tip of the Chromosome." *American Journal of Psychiatry* 178(2): 113–115.

169 von Zglinicki, T. 2002. "Oxidative Stress Shortens Telomeres." *Trends in Biochemical Sciences* 27(7), 339–344.

170 Jacobs, T. L., E. S. Epel, J. Lin, E. H. Blackburn, O. M. Wolkowitz, D. A. Bridwell, et al. 2011. "Intensive Meditation Training, Immune Cell Telomerase Activity, and Psychological Mediators." *Psychoneuroendocrinology* 36(5): 664–681.

171 Ishikawa, N., K. Nakamura, N. Izumiyama-Shimomura, J. Aida, Y. Matsuda, T. Arai, et al. 2016. "Changes of Telomere Status and Aging: An Update." *Geriatrics Gerontology International* 16(1): 30–42 Suppl.

172 O'Donovan, A., M. S. Pantell, E. Puterman, F. S. Dhabhar, E. H. Blackburn, K. Yaffe, et al. 2011. "Cumulative Inflammatory Load Is Associated with Short Leukocyte Telomere Length in the Health, Aging, and Body Composition Study." *PLOS ONE* 6(5): e19687.

173 von Zglinicki. "Oxidative Stress Shortens Telomeres."

174 Blackburn, E., & E. Epel. 2017. *The Telomere Effect: A Revolutionary Approach to Living Younger, Healthier, Longer.* New York: Grand Central Publishing.

175 Mendioroz, M., M. Puebla-Guedea, J. Montero-Marín, A. Urdánoz-Casado, I. Blanco-Luquin, M. Roldán, et al. 2020. "Telomere Length Correlates with Subtelomeric DNA Methylation in Long-Term Mindfulness Practitioners." *Scientific Reports* 10(1): 4564.

176 Lewis, E. J., K. L. Yoon, & J. Joormann. 2018. "Emotion Regulation, and Biological Stress Responding: Associations with Worry, Rumination, and Reappraisal." *Cognition and Emotion* 32: 1487–1498.

177 Raio, C. M., T. A. Orederu, L. Palazzolo, A. A. Shurick, & E. A. Phelps. 2013. "Cognitive Emotion Regulation Fails the Stress Test." *Proceedings of the National Academy of Sciences USA* 110(37): 15139–15144.

178 Frankl, V. E. 1985. *Man's Search for Meaning.* New York: Simon & Schuster.

179 Mohr, D. C., C. Stiles-Shields, C. Brenner, H. Palac, E. Montague, S. M. Kaiser, et al. 2015. "MedLink: A Mobile Intervention to Address Failure Points in the Treatment of Depression in General Medicine." 9th International Conference on Pervasive Computing Technologies for Healthcare (*PervasiveHealth*), Istanbul, Turkey, 2015: 100–107.

180 Kato, M., H. Hori, T. Inoue, J. Iga, M. Iwata, T. Inagaki, et al. 2021. "Discontinuation of Antidepressants after Remission with Antidepressant Medication in Major Depressive Disorder: A Systematic Review and Meta-Analysis." *Molecular Psychiatry* 26(1): 118–133.

181 Steinert, C., M. Hofmann, J. Kruse, & F. Leichsenring. 2014. "Relapse Rates after Psychotherapy for Depression—Stable Long-Term Effects? A Meta-Analysis." *Journal of Affective Disorders* 168: 107–118.

182 Nierenberg, A. A., T. J. Petersen, & J. E. Alpert. 2003. "Prevention of Relapse and Recurrence in Depression: The Role of Long-Term Pharmacotherapy and Psychotherapy." *Journal of Clinical Psychiatry* 64(15): 13–17.

183 Ruini, C., E. Albieri, & F. Vescovelli. 2015. "Well-Being Therapy: State of the Art and Clinical Exemplifications." *Journal of Contemporary Psychotherapy* 45(2): 129–136.

184 Ryff, C. D. 2014. "Psychological Well-Being Revisited: Advances in the Science and Practice of Eudaimonia." *Psychotherapy and Psychosomatics* 83(1): 10–28.

185 Guidi, J., & G. A. Fava. 2021. "Conceptual and Clinical Innovations of Well-Being Therapy." *Journal of Cognitive Therapy* 14: 196–208.

186 Merlo, E. M., A. P. Stoian, I. G. Motofei, & S. Settineri. 2021. "The Role of Suppression and the Maintenance of Euthymia in Clinical Settings." *Frontiers in Psychology* 12: 677811.

Chapter 6

187 Ray, J. 2022. "World Unhappier, More Stressed Out Than Ever." *Gallup*, June 28, 2022. https://ncws.gallup.com/poll/394025/world -unhappier-stressed-ever.aspx.

188 Kibbel III, W. n.d. "Common Fire Safety Device in Old Homes a Health Hazard." *Old House Web.* https://www.oldhouseweb.com /how-to-advice/common-fire-safety-device-in-old-homes-a-health -hazard.shtml.

189 Spielmans, G. I., T. Spence-Sing, & P. Parry. 2020. "Duty to Warn: Antidepressant Black Box Suicidality Warning Is Empirically Justified." *Frontiers in Psychiatry* 11: 18.

190 Anthes, E. 2014. "Depression: A Change of Mind." *Nature* 515: 185–187.

191 Ormel, J., S. D. Hollon, R. C. Kessler, P. Cuijpers, & S. M. Monroe. 2022. "More Treatment but No Less Depression: The Treatment– Prevalence Paradox." *Clinical Psychology Review* 91: 102111.

192 Barry, E. 2022. "A Mental Health Clinic in School? No, Thanks, Says the School Board." *The New York Times,* June 7th, 2020. https://www.nytimes.com/2022/06/05/health/killingly-ct-mental -health-clinic-school.html.

193 Pandey, A., D. Hale, S. Das, A. L. Goddings, S. J. Blakemore, & R. M. Viner. 2018. "Effectiveness of Universal Self-Regulation–Based Interventions in Children and Adolescents: A Systematic Review and Meta-Analysis." *JAMA Pediatrics* 172(6): 566–575.

194 Paschall, M. J., & M. Bersamin. 2017. "School-Based Mental Health Services, Suicide Risk and Substance Use among At-Risk Adolescents in Oregon." *Preventive Medicine* 106: 209–215.

195 Barry, E. "A Mental Health Clinic in School?"

196 Bakker, A. B., & J. D. de Vries 2021. "Job Demands–Resources Theory and Self-Regulation: New Explanations and Remedies for Job Burnout." *Anxiety, Stress, & Coping* 34(1): 1–21.

197 Luthans, F., & C. M. Youssef-Morgan. 2017. "Psychological Capital: An Evidence-Based Positive Approach." *Annual Review of Organizational Psychology and Organizational Behavior* 4: 339–366.

198 Finch, J., L. J. Farrell, & A. M. Waters. 2020. "Searching for the HERO in Youth: Does Psychological Capital (PsyCap) Predict Mental Health Symptoms and Subjective Well-Being in Australian School-Aged Children and Adolescents?" *Child Psychiatry & Human Development* 51(6): 1025–1036.

199 Oettingen, G. 2012. "Future Thought and Behaviour Change." *European Review of Social Psychology* 23: 1–63.

200 Duckworth, A. L., H. Grant, B. Loew, G. Oettingen, & P. M. Gollwitzer. 2011. "Self-Regulation Strategies Improve Self-Discipline in Adolescents: Benefits of Mental Contrasting and Implementation Intentions." *Education Psychology* 31: 17–26.

201 Tedeschi, R. G., & L. G. Calhoun. 2004. "Posttraumatic Growth: Conceptual Foundations and Empirical Evidence." *Psychological Inquiry* 15(1): 1–18.

202 Jayawickreme, E., F. J. Infurna, K. Alajak, L. E. Blackie, W. J. Chopik, J. M. Chung, et al. 2021. "Post-traumatic Growth as Positive Personality Change: Challenges, Opportunities, and Recommendations." *Journal of Personality* 89(1): 145–165.

203 Dekel, S., I. T. Hankin, J. A. Pratt, D. R. Hackler, &
O. N. Lanman. 2016. "Posttraumatic Growth in Trauma
Recollections of 9/11 Survivors: A Narrative Approach."
Journal of Loss and Trauma 21(4): 315–324.

204 Kin. n.d. "100-Year Floodplain." https://www.kin.com/glossary
/100-year-floodplain/#:~:text=The%20100-year%20flood%20is
%20simply%20one%20way%20of,100-year%20flood%20is%20
also%20called%20the%20base%20flood.

205 Taku, K., R. G. Tedeschi, J. Shakespeare-Finch, D. Krosch,
G. David, D. Kehl, et al. 2021. "Posttraumatic Growth (PTG)
and Posttraumatic Depreciation (PTD) Across Ten Countries:
Global Validation of the PTG-PTD Theoretical Model."
Personality and Individual Differences 169(1): 110222.

206 Tedeschi & Calhoun. "Posttraumatic Growth: Conceptual
Foundations and Empirical Evidence."

207 Zacher, H., & U. M. Staudinger. 2018. "Wisdom and Well-Being."
In *Handbook of Well-Being*, edited by E. Diener, S. Oishi, & L. Tay.
Salt Lake City: DEF Publishers.

208 Tedeschi & Calhoun. "Posttraumatic Growth: Conceptual
Foundations and Empirical Evidence."

209 Taku et al. "Posttraumatic Growth (PTG) and Posttraumatic
Depreciation (PTD) Across Ten Countries: Global Validation of
the PTG–PTD Theoretical Model."

210 Dekel et al. "Posttraumatic Growth in Trauma Recollections of
9/11 Survivors."

211 Pollari, C. D., J. Brite, R. M. Brackbill, L. M. Gargano,
S. W. Adams, P. Russo-Netzer, et al. 2021. "World Trade
Center Exposure and Posttraumatic Growth: Assessing Positive
Psychological Change 15 Years after 9/11." *International Journal
of Environmental Research and Public Health* 18(1): 104.

212 Vallerand, R. J. 2015. *The Psychology of Passion: A Dualistic Model*.
Oxford: Oxford University Press.

213 Vallerand, R. J., G. A. Mageau, A. J. Elliot, A. Dumais,
M. A. Demers, & F. Rousseau. 2008. "Passion and Performance
Attainment in Sport." *Psychology of Sport and Exercise* 9(3): 373–392.

214 Vallerand et al. "Passion and Performance Attainment in Sport."

215 Zhang, S. E., S. A. Ge, J. Tian, Q. L. Li, M. S. Wang, X. H. Wang,
et al. 2022. "A Cross-Sectional Study of Individual Learning Passion
in Medical Education: Understanding Self-Development
in Positive Psychology." *Frontiers in Psychology* 13: 758002.

216 Lavoie, C. E., R. J. Vallerand, & J. Verner-Filion. 2021. "Passion
and Emotions: The Mediating Role of Cognitive Appraisals."
Psychology of Sport and Exercise 54: 101907.

217 Kaufmann, S. B. 2011. "How to Increase Your Harmonious Passion."
September 26, 2011. https://scottbarrykaufman.com/how-to-increase
-your-harmonious-passion.

218 Lafrenière, M-A. K., J. J. Bélanger, C. Sedikides, & R. J. Vallerand.
2011. "Self-Esteem and Passion for Activities." *Personality and
Individual Differences* 51(4): 541–544.

219 Burke, S. M., C. M. Sabiston, & R. J. Vallerand. 2012. "Passion
in Breast Cancer Survivors: Examining Links to Emotional
Well-Being." *Journal of Health Psychology* 17(8): 1161–1175.

220 Burke, Sabiston, & Vallerand. "Passion in Breast Cancer Survivors."

Chapter 7

221 Gardiner, G., K. Sauerberger, D. Lee, & D. Funder. 2022. "What
Happy People Do: The Behavioral Correlates of Happiness in
Everyday Situations." *Journal of Research in Personality* 99: 104236.

222 Sytine, A. I., T. W. Britt, G. Sawhney, C. A. Wilson, & M. Keith.
2019. "Savoring as a Moderator of the Daily Demands and
Psychological Capital Relationship: A Daily Diary Study."
The Journal of Positive Psychology 14(5): 641–648.

223 Fredrickson, B. L., & T. Joiner. 2018. "Reflections on Positive
Emotions and Upward Spirals." *Perspectives on Psychological Science*
13(2): 194–199.

Dan Tomasulo, PhD, is author of the popular self-help guide, *Learned Hopefulness*, hailed as "the perfect recipe for fulfillment, joy, peace, and expansion of awareness" by Deepak Chopra. He is core faculty at the Spirituality Mind Body Institute (SMBI) at Teachers College, Columbia University; and was honored by Sharecare as one of the top ten online influencers on the issue of depression. He holds a PhD in psychology, an MFA in writing, and a master of applied positive psychology from the University of Pennsylvania. A highly sought-after international speaker on topics relating to applied positive psychology, he authors the popular blog, *The Healing Crowd*, for *Psychology Today*. His award-winning memoir, *American Snake Pit*, was released in 2018.

Foreword writer **Lisa Miller, PhD**, is professor in the clinical psychology program at Teachers College, Columbia University, where she founded the Spirituality Mind Body Institute—the first Ivy League graduate program in spirituality and psychology. She is author of *The Awakened Brain* and *The Spiritual Child*.

Real change *is* possible

For more than forty-five years, New Harbinger has
published proven-effective self-help books and pioneering
workbooks to help readers of all ages and backgrounds
improve mental health and well-being, and achieve lasting
personal growth. In addition, our spirituality books
offer profound guidance for deepening awareness and
cultivating healing, self-discovery, and fulfillment.

Founded by psychologist Matthew McKay and Patrick
Fanning, New Harbinger is proud to be an independent,
employee-owned company. Our books reflect our
core values of integrity, innovation, commitment,
sustainability, compassion, and trust. Written by leaders
in the field and recommended by therapists worldwide,
New Harbinger books are practical, accessible, and
provide real tools for real change.

 **newharbinger**publications

MORE BOOKS from
NEW HARBINGER PUBLICATIONS

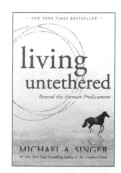

LIVING UNTETHERED

Beyond the Human
Predicament

978-1648480935 / US $18.95

PUT YOUR ANXIETY HERE

A Creative Guided Journal to
Relieve Stress and Find Calm

978-1648481451 / US $18.95

**50 WAYS TO
SOOTHE YOURSELF
WITHOUT FOOD**

978-1572246768 / US $18.95

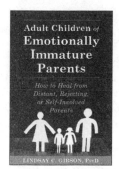

**ADULT CHILDREN
OF EMOTIONALLY
IMMATURE PARENTS**

How to Heal from
Distant, Rejecting, or
Self-Involved Parents

978-1626251700 / US $18.95

**YOUR COPING SKILLS
AREN'T WORKING**

How to Break Free from the
Habits that Once Helped You
But Now Hold You Back

978-1648480997 / US $18.95

BUDDHA'S BRAIN

The Practical Neuroscience of
Happiness, Love, and Wisdom

978-1572246959 / US $18.95

newharbingerpublications
1-800-748-6273 / newharbinger.com

(VISA, MC, AMEX / prices subject to change without notice)
Follow Us 🅾 📘 🎦 ▶ 📌 in

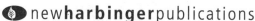